The VERMONT
Owner's Manual

The VERMONT
Owner's Manual

Frank Bryan
Bill Mares

Illustrated by Jeff Danziger

The New England Press, Inc.
Shelburne, Vermont

FB—To my sister Jane. Vermont awaits.
WM—To my sons Tim and Nick. At least *they* were born here.

First edition
Manufactured in the United States of America
ISBN 1-881535-40-1
Library of Congress Catalog Card Number: 00-109744

For additional copies of this book or for a catalog of
our other titles, please write:

The New England Press
P.O. Box 575
Shelburne, VT 05482

or e-mail nep@together.net

Visit our Web site at www.nepress.com

Contents

Acknowledgments .... *viii*

Freedom and *Unity* .... *ix*

Congratulations .... *x*

The Bug .... *xii*

Leasing Agreement .... *xiii*

1. Fence Pliers and Jumper Cables 1
   (Your Vermont Tool Kit)
2. Comments of Previous Owners 5
3. The Green Pages 6
   (A Generic Vermont Phone Book)
4. Ground Hog Day 8
   (And Other Important Dates on
   Your Vermont Calendar)
5. The Anarchy of Cussedness 14
   (Understanding Vermont Politics)
6. The Vermont Manifesto 17
7. Are You Ready to Operate Vermont? 18
   (Quiz #1)
8. Talkin' Chuck 20
9. Talkin' "Lander" 24
10. Warm Februarys and Hornets' Nests 27
    (Things to Avoid at All Costs)

11. The Profanity Page 29

12. Comments of Previous Owners 31

13. Snowflake Bentley 32
    and Other Braggin' Rights

14. Are You Ready to Operate Vermont? 38
    (Quiz #2)

15. Foggy Mountain Breakdown 40
    (Operating the Public Schools)

16. Who Ya Gonna Call? 47
    (Understanding the Chain of Command)

17. The Education Rules 49

18. The Act 60 Page 51

19. Sacred Cows and Baler Twine 52
    (Living with the Farmers)

20. Comments of Previous Owners 59

21. The "High Chair" Treatment 61
    (Crime and Punishment)

22. Green Up Daze 66

23. The Politicians 71
    (Who Should You Let Operate Your Vermont?)

24. Surviving Deer Season 74

25. Are You Ready to Operate Vermont? 77
    (Quiz #3)

26. Yeas and Nays 79
    (Coping with Town Meeting)

27. Comments of Previous Owners 87

28. Governors and Hog Reeves 89
    (Who do you vote for?)

29. Neighbors 92

30. What Do You DO Up There? 95
31. Flatlander Syndrome 97
    (Recognizing the Early Warning Signs)
32. Are You *Finally* Set to Operate Vermont? . 102
    (Quiz #4)
33. "The Gods of the Hills" 104
    (Your Vermont Warranty)
34. Safety Features 105
35. Optional Features and Spare Parts............ 107
36. The Vermont Weather Page 109
37. Don't Brake for Field Mice! 111
    (The Commuter Rules)
38. The Best of Everything 114
39. Comments of Visitors and 118
    "Summer People"
40. The Media Page 120
41. Vermont Political Correctness 122
42. Which Road to Take? 125

Acknowledgments

We would like to thank some people for their contribution(s) to this book. We're Vermonters, so we'll skip the flowery details, but we appreciate the help provided by each and every person in the following list:

Russ Aceto; Sherry Bigelow; Al Boright; Marie Bremser; Paul Bruhn; David Bryan; Jennifer Bryan; Melissa Bryan; Jack Candon; Kay Church; John and Patsy Cole; Jim Condon; Hamilton Davis; Dick Drysdale; Marie Eddy; Jack Ewell; Jan Feldman; Ruby Fern; Ann Fisher; Jacob Fournier; Peter Freyne; The Goldricks; Joe Grunwald; Chris Hadsel; Christian Henricksen; Jeff Hinds; Rick Imes; Mark Johnson; Sally Johnson; Jane and Eddie Krasnow; David Larsen; Louie Manno; Joanne Moore; Steve Morris; Travis Morrison; Stella Moyser; Jean Osborn; Lloyd Portnow; Al and Maggie Rosa; Norm Runnion; Tom Slayton; Bob Smith; Sylvia Jarvis Smith; Ralph Swenson; Mark Wanner; Selenda Whitney; and Art Woolf.

Freedom and *Unity*

Back in the 1980s we wrote *Real Vermonters Don't Milk Goats*. It went through six printings—one copy for every ten men, women, and children in Vermont. Had it been a national book, we'd have sold more than 20,000,000 copies and become very, very rich.

But this is Vermont. Wealth is not in God's plan up here.

So we focused on the fun and the friends we made.

Now things are different. The tension that sparked *Goats* flashed between poles marked "newcomer" and "native." In our personal lives, we sit on those distant poles. One of us is a *'lander*, the other's a *chuck*. Perhaps our friendship can be a model for preserving dear things fraught with contradictions.[1]

Like Vermont.

[1] Vermont is full of contradictions. Even its motto (Freedom and Unity) is an oxymoron.

Congratulations!

There is no more Yankee than Polynesian in me. But when I go to Vermont, I feel like I am traveling toward my own place.

—Bernard DeVoto

Vermont. Ten thousand square miles of pastured forest over granite hills between the wide lake and the long river; the crankiest, smartest, toughest, liberty-lovingest commonwealth of tolerance in the Western Hemisphere; with a history to warm the soul, a land to please the senses, a people to love. And best of all:

THIS IS YOUR PLACE. YOU OWN IT. ALL OF IT.

It doesn't belong to Howard Dean or Jim Jeffords. It doesn't belong to Bernie Sanders or Pat Leahy. Sure they're owners. But, hell, we're all owners. They work for us. That's the neat thing about town meeting or a polling booth. Once inside, everyone's equal.

Vermont doesn't belong to IBM or Ben & Jerry's or Green Mountain Power or the ACLU or the National Education Association or the Vermont Landowners Association or the Vermont Supreme Court or the National Rifle

Association. It doesn't belong to Michael Obuchowski or Vincent Iluzzi or Doug Racine or Cheryl Rivers. It doesn't belong to the Environmental Board or the Vermont Ski Owners Association, to Planned Parenthood or Vermont Right to Life, to the *Rutland Herald*, the *Burlington Free Press,* or WCAX Television. American troubadour Woody Guthrie had it right!

THIS LAND BELONGS TO YOU AND ME.

But Vermont is not just land. It's everything. Vermont isn't what it looks like. It's what its people are. It's us. And we have to care for ourselves, our Vermont.

Our *common*wealth.

There was a time when living the Vermont life was not *second* nature to us; it was *first* nature. Times have changed. Living in Vermont is like operating a new piece of sophisticated machinery. It's understanding that controversy is the oxygen of democracy, that cows and manure go together, that *looking* country and *being* country are not the same, that city solutions to rural problems don't work, that political correctness in a liberal society is water in the gas, that good fences do, by god, make better neighbors.

The Bug

Several decades ago a strange looking foreign car crossed the Atlantic. It was small. It was quirky. It was unique; stick shift, motor in the back, bucket seats. It was frugal. It was high tech. It was owned by individualists who didn't give a damn how their car looked or what other people thought about it. In an era of chrome and fins and horsepower, it was as different from other automobiles as Vermont is now from the rest of America.

Those who owned it knew at once they had an ornery little devil on their hands. It took special skills to drive. It took a special way of thinking about cars and transportation and, in fact, life itself. Suddenly you were not driving *in* a car, you were driving *with* a car. It became apparent that such a vehicle begged for a *special* owner's manual. So somebody wrote one.

Of course, Vermont isn't a car. (In fact, lots of Vermonters think there are too many of them here already.) Neither is it a chain saw, a sailboat, a computer, or a snowmobile. But like these and lots of other special good things Vermont needs to be taken care of and treated right. It's our most prized possession. It's our home.

Vermont today is like the Bug of yesterday. It needs an owner's manual too.

Before we get started, though,
perhaps you'd be interested in:

The Vermont Owner's Manual

Leasing Agreement

(An Alternative to Ownership)

For those readers who do not wish to assume the
responsibility for the care and maintenance of Vermont
that living here requires but would like to use it under
a special leasing agreement, please turn the page for
details.

The Vermont Owner's Manual
Leasing Agreement:
An Alternative to Ownership
(Continued from page *xiii*)

If you are seriously considering leasing Vermont, we have a quick question to ask before you proceed further.

ARE YOU NUTS?

Are you related to Jack McMullen, the carpetbagger Fred Tuttle put in his place in 1998? Was some obscure and distant branch of your family tree grafted to that of Hillary Clinton? Whattaya think this is, *New York*?

You can't just show up! You can't *use* Vermont and then give it back. If you intend to live here and to *vote* here, you must be an owner. It takes some commitment, sure. But so does anything else of value. Take the plunge or stay on the shore! We don't want any toe-dippers here.

This doesn't mean you can't spend the summer. It doesn't mean you can't visit. You can peep at leaves or "hunt 'n fish" or antique or snowmobile to your heart's content.

Just don't forget to bring cash.

1

Fence Pliers and Jumper Cables
(Your Vermont Tool Kit)

Tools. Vermonters pride themselves on their ability to "make do" with as few as possible. That is why duct tape sells so well. It also explains Bag Balm and bailing twine. Nevertheless, from time to time you may have to do some repair work on Vermont. Here are the tools to have handy.

- A fishing pole.[2]
- A copy of Robert's Rules of Order.
- The capacity to grin and bear it.[3]
- Hope.
- Needle-nosed pliers.
- Directions back to New Jersey.
- Tolerance.
- A 12-gauge shotgun.

[2] In case you can't fix the problem.

[3] In case you forgot your fishing pole.

Don't forget your capacity to grin and bear it.

🔻 Bug repellent.

🔻 A copy of the Vermont Constitution.[4]

🔻 The willingness to live and let live.

🔻 A chainsaw file.

🔻 Mittens.

🔻 Governor Dean's phone number.[5]

🔻 Jumper cables.

🔻 Boots in the trunk.

🔻 A plumber's friend.

🔻 A second source of income.

🔻 A bright orange hat.

Remember, no good Vermont tool kit contains any extra stuff. So here are a few items you will *never* need.

🔻 Shitake mushrooms.

🔻 A fanny pack.

🔻 Martha Stewart.

🔻 *Home and Garden* magazine.

🔻 HOV lanes.[6]

---

[4] Not, however, the secret Constitution that the Vermont State Supreme Court uses.

[5] If you can't find it in the phone book, call the Republican State Committee in Montpelier. He lives there half the time anyway.

[6] Old-time Vermonters may want or need an acronym dictionary in their tool box.

- Gregariousness.

- Fire starter logs.

- A Ph.D. in Political Science.[7]

- A fitness trainer.

- Sun block.

- Howard Stern.

- Beach volleyball.

- The Weather Channel.

- Aromatherapy.

- Black ties.

- Summer tires.

- Extra G's to use on gerunds.[8]

- A global positioning system.[9]

- e-commerce.

- Pre-nuptial agreements.

[7] In Vermont, political science is another oxymoron.

[8] Thus if you find yourself saying "goin' fishin'," Vermonters won't mind. You need no replacements in your tool kit.

[9] Actually newcomers might need one for their foliage excursions.

2

Comments of Previous Owners

These principles of loving liberty, of self reliance, of thrift and of liberalism have inspired Vermonters to the greatest, most satisfying of all ideals—self-respect. We are not ashamed. We do not think it old-fashioned or reactionary to insist upon the principle of local self-government. We believe that local control of government is not antiquated but progressive.

George Aiken, Putney

The record of Vermont as a resolute champion of individual freedom, as a true interpreter of our fundamental law, as a defender of religious faith, as a unselfish but independent and uncompromising commonwealth of liberty-loving patriots, is not only unsurpassed but unmatched by any other state in the Union.

George Harvey, Peacham

I shall do everything in my power to render this state a British Province.

Ethan Allen, Colchester

3

The Green Pages
(A Generic Vermont Phone Book)

VOM could give you the key phone numbers you need to help operate your Vermont. But what's the point? You'll want your own list. Here are some suggestions to get you started.

Phone Number

The "Moose in Your Garden" Hotline. _____

A mechanic you can count
on to inspect your "parts" car. _____

Your neighbor. (To ask them if
their power's off too.) _____

A veterinarian who will give your
dog its rabies shot without making
you feel guilty for not spending
$1,742.86 to kill the fleas.[10] _____

A real Vermonter who owns a
pickup truck.[11] _____

A plumber who will thaw pipes
for less than $125 an hour. _____

[10] Or $2,500 for six weekly sessions of joint canine counseling
for you and your dog.

[11] With plow.

6

Your state legislator.[12]   _____

The principal of your local high school.[13]   _____

A satellite dish repairman.   _____

Someone who likes zucchini—**big** ones.   _____

WDEV radio station.[14]   _____

Someone who can prune apple trees.   _____

A real estate dealer in Sarasota, Florida.[15]   _____

[12] Not that it'll matter much.

[13] It will most likely be a long distance call.

[14] In case you have to sell something.

[15] Heck, up in this neck of the woods, everyone gets discouraged from time to time.

4

Ground Hog Day
(And Other Important Dates on Your Vermont Calendar)

Vermont needs its own calendar. You may be able to get along with a standard version in the other forty-nine states but in Vermont you'll miss out on a lot of the good stuff if you don't keep track of its special days. Even the old American standbys take on a different meaning in a place where you are at the mercy of the seasons.

NEW YEAR'S DAY

In Vermont the first day of the new year is April 23 or the first time a farmer can sink his plow into the ground any place north of Hardwick, whichever comes first. This starts the cycle. Like oak trees and bears, Vermonters live by a simple truth— life is one long preparation for winter.

MAY DAY

Step out on the porch, pat the dog, and heave a huge sigh of relief. April, which has been promising paradise and delivering hell for thirty days, is at last over.

GREEN UP DAY

Vermonters clean up a place on the front lawn for another used car or boat. Flatlanders clean up alongside the road.[16]

---

[16] Some give up immediately. Appalled.

May Day

MOTHER'S DAY

In Vermont we honor our mothers. (And plant the peas.)

MEMORIAL DAY

There is a little graveyard in southern Vermont. Every year there comes an old woman. She lays her flowers on the ground and stands to see where the lilacs still mark the clearing's edge. On the stone it says: "Died in Normandy, France. June 24, 1944."

SUMMER SOLSTICE

The longest day of the year (June 21) is the *best* day of the year in Vermont and therefore the *worst*. The truth of June 21 is this: from that day on every day gets shorter.

4TH OF JULY

Dig out the flag and hang it on the porch. Pick some peas for dinner. (You did plant them on Mother's Day, right?) Head into town for the parade. (Don't forget change for the coin drop.) On the way home stop for some chips and beer. Hitch up the dogs before the neighbors get there for the barbecue. For once try to leave for the fireworks in time to get a decent parking place. And don't feel so guilty! Even Vermonters get to relax once in awhile.

BENNINGTON BATTLE DAY

Ignore it. Everyone else does.[17]

LABOR DAY

Work like hell. Winter's coming.

THE FIRST FROST COMES TO CANAAN

It is there, hovering somewhere over James Bay. The cold. On

---

[17] Except state employees, of course.

this day all real Vermonters begin to think like the folk singer Judy Collins:

Across the morning sky all the birds are leaving
Oh how can they know—it's time for them to go
Before a winter's fire we'll still be dreaming
I do not fear the time
I do not fear the time

THE FIRST DAY OF DEER SEASON

Stay in the house with the shades drawn. Either that or get out on a stand at dawn. It's safe there too. And you may get to watch a cold sun flash through a frozen forest and turn the world to gold. Or you may just freeze your ass off.

THANKSGIVING

Remember this: Even Dunkin' Donuts is closed! Here is a generic Vermont turkey blessing in case you need one:

Bless this turkey, oh Lord, and all the other turkeys
in the state—many of whom are relatives. Bless the
game warden for being on the other side of town
when I shot this baby out of season. We call your
attention to Uncle Charlie and ask you to help him
find his way out of Victory Bog where he went
hunting last Tuesday. And yet again we ask you to
repeal the statewide property tax. Finally, as we
partake of the bounty this great state has delivered,
keep us from chomping down on any of the No. 2
shot with which I blew this magnificent bird off the
top of Wayne Wheeler's manure pile.

CHRISTMAS

For advice on how to celebrate Christmas, turn to page 63.

NEW YEAR'S DAY

Turn to late April.

JANUARY 4

This is the *worst* day of the year in Vermont and therefore the *best*. It is often 20 below and cold white covers every horizon. But Vermonters know something very important. It is a teensy bit lighter at 4:00 p.m. than it was on January 3rd.

GROUND HOG DAY

Vermonters, especially, welcome the appearance of the first "woodchuck." The best thing about Ground Hog Day is that it's only a month from Town Meeting Day, which is only a month from trout season. Vermont is one-third nostalgia and two-thirds hope.

VALENTINE'S DAY

Flatlanders and real Vermonters meet and exchange gifts.[18]

---

[18] Flatlanders give Vermonters things like *A Guide to the Long Trail* while Vermonters give flatlanders things like a hand warmer for their snowmobile. Both throw them away as soon as they get home.

TOWN MEETING DAY

Go. (And plant your tomatoes.)

APRIL FOOL'S DAY

Real Vermonters call flatlanders and tell them "Vermont Public Radio just went bankrupt." Flatlanders call real Vermonters and say "Thunder Road International Speedway has been converted into a llama farm."

EASTER

If you're going to a "sunrise" service in Vermont in early April, you must really be a true believer. All the more power to you. Our advice: Trust in the Lord, but take your boots.

THE FIRST DAY OF TROUT SEASON

This is the last day of the year in Vermont. The sap's dried up. Mud season is over,[19] and the hardwood hills seem fuzzy in the late afternoon. You've wintered again. Celebrate. Take some night crawlers out of the fridge, put them in a frost-proof can, grab some mittens, and go fishing.

---

[19] South of the Winooski, anyway.

5

The Anarchy of Cussedness

(Understanding Vermont Politics)[20]

The bottom line? Vermonters don't care what the state does as long as it's different. Vermont was *created* a contradiction—a cultural oxymoron. Thus our state motto is "Freedom *and* Unity." Ethan Allen slapped Vermont politics into life with the enigmatic declaration: "The Gods of the Hills are not the Gods of the Valleys." To which Vermonters say:

"You bet!"[21]

Vermont elected one of the most cantankerous Congressmen in history, Matthew Lyon. He was in jail in Vergennes when elected. (Nowadays, people are elected

---

[20] This description of Vermont is immortalized in the title of Ralph Nading Hill's splendid book, *Contrary Country*. Hill is responsible for the only hypothesis to bear fruit in the history of 20th Century social science. In 1950 he wrote "If the rest of the states went Republican, that would be the day Vermont would go Democratic." He nailed it!

[21] Even though they haven't the slightest idea what Ethan meant.

to Congress and *then* go to jail.) Vermonters figured that being sent to jail (Lyons called the President of the United States some unpleasant names) was no reason not to send him to Washington.

When the Democrats and liberals controlled the nation from 1932 through 1968 Vermont was the most Republican state in America. By far!

When Americans marched off to the right with Ronald Reagan, Vermonters passed them going the other way and became the last stand of liberalism.

In the 1950s, when America slipped into the darkness of McCarthyism, Vermont stood firm in the sunlight of decency.

In the election of 1994, when every defeated incumbent in the House of Representatives was a Democrat, Vermont upped the ante and returned a socialist! We'll do anything to be different. Even vote for Bernie.[22]

---

[22] When Socialist Sanders was elected mayor of Burlington about the time Socialist Francois Mitterand became president of France, cartoonist Gary Trudeau proclaimed in a Doonesbury cartoon, "As goes Burlington, so goes France."

This explains why:

- ▼ Howard Dean is really a Republican.

- ▼ There ain't gonna be no McDonald's in Montpelier!

- ▼ We are one of only two states that has kept its two-year term for governor.

- ▼ Jim Jeffords is really a Democrat.

- ▼ We refused to pass an Equal Rights Amendment to our own Constitution. We intended to. Heck, we wanted to. Then a bunch of pollsters had to go and predict we would!

- ▼ In 1989, seven Vermont towns were given the opportunity to vote on whether to secede from the Union or celebrate joining it. They all voted OUT!

- ▼ The most liberal American state has one of the planet's most archaic set of gun laws.

6

The Vermont Manifesto

*Is there a "lost cause"? Then I am for it. Is there a philosophy of life and destiny weak and rejected of men? Then will I examine and tolerate and, if needs be, defend that philosophy in its extremity . . . Yes, write me down as one who abhors a sham, one who resists limitations, who despises cant; as one who will condemn repression and intolerance of every sort . . . who, for these reasons, and because of an inherent tendency of personality, was ever, and will ever be, **one of the minority**.*[23]

---

[23] Penned by Walter Coates, a "hill town writer," and immortalized by Ralph Nading Hill.

7

Are You Ready to Operate Vermont?

Quiz #1

1. Which of the following was *not* a Vermont "first"?
    - (A) State to pass a "bottle bill" to cut down on roadside litter.
    - (B) American governmental body to declare war on Japan in 1941.
    - (C) State to ban the Communist Party from appearing on the ballot.
    - (D) State to offer a course in air traffic regulation.
    - (E) All of the above.

2. Everyone knows that the Vermont official state flower is the red clover.[24] But do you know the official Vermont state fruit?
    - (A) Blueberry.
    - (B) Chokecherry.
    - (C) Jim Jeffords.
    - (D) Road Apple.
    - (E) None of the above.

---

[24] Actually, some Vermonters argue it ought to be the satellite dish.

18

3. Which song did the legislature accept as the official state song?

(A) The Cajun hit of the mid 1970s "Dead Skunk in the Middle of the Road."

(B) "These Green Mountains."

(C) "Night Train to Shelburne" (by Howard Dean).

(D) "Little White Lies" (The Vermont Supreme Court's entry).

(E) "Moonlight in Vermont."

4. Which of the following did the legislature recently designate as the official state pie?

(A) chicken pot

(B) pumpkin

(C) cow[25]

(D) apple

(E) 3.14[26]

Answers: 1. C 2. E 3. B 4. D

[25] This was actually proposed as an amendment to the official pie bill. Unfortunately it was defeated.

[26] Any graduates of a Vermont high school who wonder about this one should sue their local school district.

8

Talkin' Chuck

In order to operate your Vermont successfully, communication is essential. Used to be that everyone understood each other *as easy as pie* (pronounced *poyee*). Now, Flatlanders and Woodchucks need *help* understanding one another.

WOODCHUCK TO FLATLANDER TRANSLATIONS

You're on a golf course and you hear someone scream *Foah*. Hit the dirt. A Vermonter with three clubs (all carried under his arm) has just teed off.

The following is a list of Talkin' Chuck instructions penned by Stephen Morris in *Vermont Sunday Magazine*.

In native Chuckese the number *nine* is pronounced *noyne* to rhyme with *groin*. The number *five* is pronounced *foyve* to rhyme with *loyve*, as in *loyve* bait. Here are a few terms and definitions so you will not be out of place at Thunder Road or the beer hall at the Tunbridge World's Fair.

Some. This all-purpose word is perhaps the most important in all Chuckdom, as it extends any other descriptive adjective. Hard to explain, but easy to demonstrate. "*Some* cold today." "That dress was *some* expensive."

Don't you know? (Sounds like, *Dontchuno*?) A phrase
without meaning used gratuitously in conversation.
Appropriate at the end of any sentence or fragment
thereof. Often used in conjunction with *some*.
Example:"*Some* cold today, *dontchuno*?"

Mother. One's wife, girlfriend or significant other (now
there is a Flatlander term!). As in "*Mother* gets *some*
peeved when I drink too many beers, *dontchuno*?"

Jeezum Crow (locally, *boi jeezum, boi the jeezum,* or
boi the jumpin' jeezum). A North Country epithet
with religious implications. Just stay out of the way
of anyone who gets to the *jumpin' jeezum* stage,
especially if he is either drunk or has a gun.

Cree-Mee. A soft ice-milk confection dispensed at
roadside stands and quick-stops in the North. Served
in several flavors, but any flavor beyond vanilla is
superfluous. *Ben & Jerry's* with their White Russian
Double Cheesecake Chocolate Cherry Chunk will
never reach this audience.[27]

Dubblewoid. A trailer, or prefabricated home, double
the normal sixteen-foot width, for many the fulfill-
ment of a life-long dream. Spelled *doublewide.*
Often seen on Interstate 89 with accompanying
signage, *WOID LOAD.*

Noice spread. An array of food at a social gathering,
including cheese cubes (Velveeta), Ritz crackers,
decorated Spam, and quart bottles of Genesee beer.

[27] Is *cree-mee* used in other states? At least one expert on Vermont,
David Sleeper (owner/editor of *Vermont Magazine*), says no.
"It isn't a *cree-mee* unless you get it at a Vermont roadside
stand."

Noice spread is a useful phrase to mutter repeatedly at a potluck dinner.

Quite a riggin' (pronounced *Kwoyt a riggin'*). Anything exceptional. Often used by males of the species to describe well-endowed females. A bad phrase to use in the presence of *Mother*.

Doodlebug. An off-road vehicle, specifically for hauling wood, often a testament to mechanical genius. Once the forward gears are stripped, one turns the seat around, and reverse becomes forward.

To Morris's list we add:

Wicked. An adjective used to denote the extreme. As in Buster was a *wicked* big bull. Or she was a *wicked* pretty girl or it was *wicked* cold. So you might have: *Jumpin' Jeezum* it was *wicked* hot, *dontchuno*.

Dickerin'. Negotiate. Often used in advertisements to indicate a price is not "firm." As in, "For sale: A *dubblewoid* trailer. *Wicked* good for snowmachines. $750. Will *dicker.* (Or swap for a *doodlebug*.)"

'...It'. Vermonters use this pronoun after they have taken the liberty of using a noun as a verb. As in: "My Uncle Walter died *farmin' it* over on the Wheeler place." Or: "Did you know his brother Walter just fell under a skidder *loggin' it* up to the Johnson lot?"[28]

---

[28] Every real Vermonter has an Uncle Walter, *dontchuno*. Documentation of this way of speech can be found in Emerson (no less), who used the phrase "*teams it*" along with "*farms it*."

Vermonters, being Yankees, don't like to talk much. That's why they speak in monosyllables. Here is a classic example from Keith Jennison's *Vermont is Where You Find It.*

> A small boy was asked, "How'd you ever find the horse everyone's been looking for, sonny?"
>
> *"I thought if I were a horse where would I go and I went and he had."*

17 words, 17 syllables. Perfect Chuckese.

David Bryan, Program Director at the Ethan Allen Homestead who holds a Ph.D. in Ancient Hittite Languages from Johns Hopkins University, agrees brevity is a key feature of Vermont language. His favorite example:

> On being asked about her upbringing in a northeastern Vermont town, a middle-aged Vermonter replied, *"Dad drank, Mom ran."*

Vermonters' passion for brevity (along with their assumption that *everyone* knows the lay of the land) means they can describe the exact topography of a trip with incredible economy by using prepositions. A Vermonter going from Greensboro Bend over the Stannard Mountain Road to Lyndonville might say:

> "I'm going *along up over around down through into* Lyndonville."

Seven prepositions and you can almost SEE the trip.

9

Talkin' "Lander"
(as in FLAT)

For their part chucks need help understanding how
flatlanders speak. For instance, flatlanders have the habit
of changing perfectly good nouns into perfectly silly
verbs, as when former Secretary of State Don Hooper
once told a conference on democracy that Vermonters
had to *neighbor* better.[29] Other examples are:

"Verbs"	Example
Task	"Let's all sit down and *task* our plans for the symposium on *Llamas on the Long Trail.*"
Effort	"Good, and while we're at it, we can *effort* the June Conference on ..."
Parent	"*Parenting* in the Clinton Age"
Dialogue	"Why don't we split up into groups of two and *dialogue* about both."
Network	"That'll work. We can *network* the date later."

[29] Vermonters lived in fear that he might really go bonkers and start
issuing proclamations like: "*Vermonters are urged to attend
town meeting next week and **democracy** their brains out.*"
Fortunately they voted him out of office before he had a chance.

To Vermont

Believe it or not a flatlander named Roger Rosenblatt changed the state into a verb! He wrote an essay on the subject and entitled it: "I Vermont, You Vermont, We Vermont." His definition: "You might say that Vermont is the emblem of a permanent human mood that is best served when it remains unsatisfied. To Vermont—it ought to be a verb (transitive)—is to not want by wanting." (Our translation: Beware of wishing for something too much—you might get it.)

His example: "The Great Gatsby *vermonted* after the bird brain Daisy, and he would have been a great deal happier, not to mention alive, if Daisy's light, like Vermont, had remained forever distant and green ..."

To New Jersey

We offer a corollary. "To New Jersey": unlike to *vermont*, to *new jersey* is to **fear** something so much you get it. We do and we have. Fortunately we seem willing to do almost all our *new jerseying* in Chittenden County.

Flatlanders also give Vermonters trouble with their use of idioms.

Idiom	Example
Outside the loop	This means you are not one of the people making the decisions. "Everyone at UVM was *outside the loop* on the hazing problem except the students." Vermonters might respond: *Bull*.

Outside the box

To do something unique and innovative, perhaps even daring. "Let's get *outside the box* on the mud season problem." (Vermonters have another phrase for most *outside the box* solutions: *damn foolishness.*)

Talking points

This refers to the critical stuff (that involve decisions and/or controversy) within tomes of obfuscation. It's kinda like: "Most of what follows is B.S. so we've summarized a few *talking points* to *task* our *dialoguing* more effectively.

Spin

To lie. Chucks lie about cordwood. Flatlanders *spin* their net worth and their place of birth.[30]

---

[30] For instance, one of the authors is a flatlander born in New Hampshire. Actually he was born in a county jail in New Hampshire. His spin on this embarrassing truth is that he was *conceived* in Vermont and according to *Roe vs. Wade* he was *brought to term* in Vermont and even *quickened* in Vermont. Therefore his birth and attendant birth certificate (which was filed in New Hampshire) is bogus. Real Vermonters think such spins are a bunch of bull, *dontchuno*.

10

Warm Februarys and Hornets' Nests

(Things to Avoid at All Costs)

With any piece of sophisticated machinery there are certain things you just don't do. The same is true for Vermont, but the danger zones are less obvious. Here are some things to keep clear of:

- ▼ Patrick Leahy making a major speech
- ▼ Taft Corners in Williston
- ▼ Hardwick during the annual Reggae Festival
- ▼ Manchester Center
- ▼ Moose in the headlights
- ▼ Republican town caucuses
- ▼ Reappraisal
- ▼ Any politician at the Tunbridge Fair
- ▼ Fancy cars from mid-Atlantic states on Route 100 in October.
- ▼ Any vehicle with a name like Navigator or Expedition.[31]

[31] A Vermonter saying, "I think I'll hop in the *Expedition* and go to town" is beyond unimaginable. Vermonters hop into *pickups* and *cars* like *Chevies* and *Hondas*. In Vermont, going to the store is **not** an expedition and doesn't require navigation!

11

The Profanity Page

To operate your Vermont you must learn the language you can get away with. All Vermonters would consider it blasphemous, for instance, to place the word "Governor" before the word "Sanders."[32] There are other, more subtle, rules. No flatlander can modify the word "salt" with the prefix "road" without revulsion. Chucks have no problem with it at all. "Wal-Mart" is a swear word for flatlanders but okay for Vermonters, who have thinner wallets.

When it gets down to hardcore blaspheme, Vermonters know Ethan Allen's is best. He was Vermont's George Washington, except that Ethan spent much of his life a brawling, drunken rascal. Accused of cutting down a cherry tree he would have said the equivalent of: "You're goddamned right I did. You got a problem with that?" When a Mr. Lee and a Mr. Stoddard, two Connecticut justices of the peace, threatened to arrest him for inoculating himself against smallpox, he gave us:

ETHAN ALLEN'S ALL-TIME BEST CURSE

By God I wish I might be bound down in hell with old Beelzabub a thousand years in the lowest pit in hell and that every little insipid devil should come along by

---

[32] "Congressman" is perfectly fine, however.

29

and ask the reason of Allen's lying there; it should be said because he made a promise on earth in cool blood that he should have the satisfaction of Lee and Stoddard and did not fulfill it!"

Ethan provided enough good cursing to last the lifetime of the state. But Vermonters have needed a generic "bad" word to get them through the day.[33] So they adopted one that sprang (perhaps oozed is a better verb) from the dominant cultural variable of state life:

SHEE-IT

This is the quintessential Vermont curse word and works in nearly every situation. However, it has several permutations. Use them as you see fit.

Bull-shee-it!	Silliness disguised (poorly) as wisdom. Often found in conjunction with the word *Montpelier.*
Horse-shee-it!	A reaction to more complicated *bull-shee-it.*
Holy-shee-it!	Used when surprised. Often in wonderment. As in *"Holy-shee-it!* Bernie's wearing a tie!"

---

[33] In addition to the more benign classics like *jeezumcrow, judaspriest,* and *crimus.* These are often used by newcomers to impress visitors from down state with the rapidity of their acclimation to Vermont. Others are *boithejesus* and *ferchrissake.*

12

Comments of Previous Owners

I came here to see how man had failed!
Down country he seems to have won all his wars;
He's littered land and befouled water.
He's a stranger to peace and the clean heart.
The fear of God is not in him.
Up here, I thought, maybe someone else
Might have the upper hand.

Vrest Orton, Sherburne

I was born in Massachusetts, educated in New Hampshire, and found peace and contentment in Vermont.

Allen R. Foley, Norwich

Certainly the ancestors of these people were wayward.
Rebellion is their birthright. Then there is the land.
There is a surprise in every turning of the various
landscape of Vermont—a mellow field, a dark woods,
a merry lake, a somber gorge, a bold mountain. And
so it is with the people. Perhaps the strength of the
hills is theirs also.

Ralph Nading Hill, Burlington

13

Snowflake Bentley and Other Braggin' Rights

When you own Vermont you own something very special. Sometimes Vermonters lose sight of this. That's easy to understand. Mass American urban culture has bombarded us with big and fast and rich for so long that it is easy to believe we have fallen so far behind we'll never "catch up."

Guess what?

We did. We won't. And who cares?

We dropped so far behind the rest of America on the racetrack of progress, we've been lapped.

NOW WE'RE AHEAD.

Did we skip the urban industrial revolution? You bet. Were we part of the technological infrastructure that fed it? You bet. Heck, we LED it. Vermont provided the brains. Pittsburgh and Chicago and the like provided the brawn. When the rest of the country indulged in the excess of the century of mass "progress" (and still wallows in the festering residues of its unhappy aftermath), we stood alone. Technologically astute, environmentally pure, and politically humane, we have emerged with our land open, our democracy intact, our communities alive, our integrity secure.

This manual contains instructions that will help us keep things this way. But it is important from time to time to pause and take note of the glories of this great state.

For instance:

The electric motor, called by scientists the most important invention of the 19th century because it allowed industry to replace steam with electricity, was invented in Brandon, Vermont.

"Snowflake" Bentley, who milked Jersey cows in Jericho, did more than photograph snow. He was a renowned world leader in the emerging science of microphotography.

In 1936 Vermont *rejected* (in a vote held in town meeting) a federal highway that would have covered the crest line of the Green Mountains from Canada to Massachusetts with blacktop. Many chuckled at this silly act of Yankee "conservatism." They didn't get it. We weren't about to glue our mountains together with asphalt. (*Dontchuno.*)

We were the ones that started the Revolutionary War. When Ethan Allen took the biggest fort in America away from the British only a few weeks after that minor scrimmage at Lexington and Concord, it was an act that couldn't be retracted. We captured something! "The British are coming. The British are coming"? Big deal! The real opening cry of the Revolution was "**Surrender in**

**the name of the Great Jehovah and the Continental
Congress!"**[34]

The most important innovation for the *marketing*
of the industrial revolution was invented in the North-
east Kingdom. It was the platform scale. By 1860 scales
built in Saint Johnsbury led the world market from
Singapore to Moscow.[35]

We won the Civil War. The day after Pickett's charge
failed during the critical Battle of Gettysburg, *The New
York Times* said that it was the Vermont Brigade that
turned the tide of the battle and thus saved the war and
the Union.

Vermont provided America's first ambassador to the
United Nations.[36]

---

[34] Allen, of course, didn't believe in "The Great Jehovah" (he
published the first anti-Christian book in North American
history) and he didn't trust the Continental Congress. Some
historians believe that his second command at Ticonderoga
(right after he demanded the unconditional surrender of the
fort) was: "And show us where you store the goddamned rum!"

[35] The impulse for the scale was agricultural. Caledonia County was
New England's leader in hemp production and growers
needed a way to market the product by a means other than
bulk measure. One might say "grass" was behind the whole
thing. The legislature might well ponder this the next time it is
asked to legalize the stuff.

[36] To wit the following: while delivering America's maiden speech
to this most progressive and most hopeful of international
organizations, former Vermont Senator Warren Austin, the crisis
area of the world being then (as it is still) the Middle East,
warned the delegates: "The Arabs and the Jews must learn to
cooperate in true Christian fashion." (*Boithejesus!*)

There are no toll roads anywhere in Vermont. None.

Vermonter Samuel Morey of Fairlee built the first carburetor equipped internal combustion engine in 1826. He also invented the steamboat, motoring across the Connecticut River in 1793. A flatlander named Fulton managed to find his way to Fairlee years later to inspect Morey's craft. Fulton finally got his running in 1806.

One of America's greatest philosophers, John Dewey, one of her greatest environmentalists, George Perkins Marsh, and one of her greatest poets, Robert Frost, were all Vermonters.[37]

Which leads us to a list of Vermont "firsts"

▼ To pass a "bottle bill."

▼ To outlaw slavery in its constitution.

▼ To prohibit billboards alongside the highways.

▼ To receive a U.S. patent.

▼ To graduate an African American from college.

▼ To elect a woman lieutenant governor.

▼ To permit absentee voting.

▼ To give the vote to people without property.

---

[37] Actually Frost was born in (yikes!) California and spent a good deal of time in New Hampshire. But he did decide to live out his days in Vermont.

▼ To establish a school of higher education for women.

▼ To have a state symphony orchestra.

▼ To have a teacher use a blackboard in class.

▼ To offer a Head Start program.

▼ To make a postage stamp used in America.

▼ To have an organized Boy Scout Club.

▼ To build a canal.

▼ To claim Federal money because it had a 6th "Great Lake."[38]

[38] This would have led to disaster. Lake Champlain is *not* a "Great Lake." It's a *real* lake. Why? Because its character (like Vermont's) is in its *smallness*. You can see the shore from the middle of the lake for heaven's sake. And the high Adirondacks and the rolling Green Mountains and harbors and inlets and little cities and villages and in many places even cows.

The 6th Great Lake?

14

Are You Ready to Operate Vermont?

Quiz #2

(A Second Check on Your Vermont Aptitude)

Vermont has a strange breed of humor. If you understand it and think it's funny (most newcomers do not) you'll know your Vermont is working just fine. To get a reading on your progress to this point see if you can provide the punch lines to several of the Vermont classics.

1. A tourist comes to a fork in the road, stops and yells to a Vermont farmer in a field about to get on his tractor. "Does it matter which road I take to get to Whitingham?"

Vermonter. "_____."

2. A traveler, having gotten out of his car, wants to cross over to the other side of a sloppy, muddy, deep-rutted, dirt road. He calls out to a Vermonter standing on the other side. "Say, how'd you get over there?"

Vermonter: "_____."

3. Downstater (trying to be nice and break the ice with her new Vermonter neighbor). "What a beautiful place you have here. Lived here all your life?"

Vermonter: "_____."

38

4. A Texan bragged to a Vermont farmer about the size of his ranch. "Why just last week I got in my truck to drive across my property and it took me the whole day."

Vermonter: "_____."

5. The following is the classic variation of the "giving directions to a newcomer" joke. All Vermonters spend their lives preparing for a chance to use it. When your opportunity comes, don't panic and blow your line. Remember. Deadpan it and then walk away without explanation.

Newcomer to Vermonter: "What is the best way to get to Grafton from here?"

Vermonter: (pause) "_____."

Answers

1. "Not to me it don't."

2. "Born here."

3. "Not yet."

4. "Had a truck like that myself once. Got rid of it."

5. You have two options:

"You can't get there from here," or

"If I was going to Grafton, I wouldn't start from here."

15

Foggy Mountain Breakdown

(Operating the Public Schools)

The proper operation of Vermont demands an understanding of its public schools.[39]

But this has been complicated by a chain reaction pile-up of educational reforms. Down the interstate of educational theory they come, bumper to bumper and careening smack into a fog bank of bureaucracy. The *basic competencies* crash into the rear end of the *public school approval process,* which plows into the *portfolio assessment movement,* which slams up against the *standards-based revolution.* For a thousand yards up and down the highway the wreckage is spewed: reports, commissions, laws, regulations, recommendations, plans and strategic plans, meetings and memos, directives, decisions, and declarations. And thousands and thousands and thousands of hours of very expensive, wasted time.

Then into this fog of perpetual chaos roars an eighteen-wheeler spewing black smoke at 76 MPH. It's Act 60!

Holy Shee-it!

---

[39] The educationalists call it an *educational system.* This, as every Vermonter knows, is like *jumbo shrimp*—an oxymoron.

The Lake Wobegon Effect

One thing not unique about Vermonters is their love for their kids. It is vital to understand, however, that Vermont has (with all the best of intentions) become a manifestation of Garrison Keillor's mythical town where all the kids are above average. On the radio it's funny—when it becomes the holy grail of Vermont's educational elite, it's still funny. But it's gallows humor. And the noose is on the neck of the schools. The following are some definitions that will help you to understand what's going on. It all adds up to schools that place self-esteem ahead of challenge and achievement.

If we get some of these definitions wrong, *so what*? At least we tried. And that's what really matters. Right?

FLEXIBLE STANDARDS

A euphemism for "do your own thing" built into education in the late 1960s and 1970s by flower people who got into the schooling thing when the revolution didn't pan out. In operation it means lowering standards again and again and again.

RUBRICS

A new system for calculating your kid's grades which establishes a hidden calculus that forces precision where precision is often inappropriate, adds to teachers' paper work when they are already swamped, confuses parents even more than they already are, challenges the teacher's ability to judge thereby striking another blow at *their* self esteeme, and further reinforces the kids' suspicions that no one knows what's going on. Otherwise it's a great idea.[40]

OUTCOME-BASED EDUCATION

Is one of two things. It could be:"It isn't how you pull the teats. It's 'did you fill the pail?'" Or, it could be:"It isn't 'did you fill the pail?' It's how you pull the teats." If you don't know which it is, don't feel bad. Nobody does.[41]

ATTENTION DEFICIT DISORDER

It's like Howard Dean's early years as governor of Vermont. Educators have recently discovered that thousands of kids have it. We cured Howard by letting him play with trains. The schools are giving your kids pills.

PORTFOLIO ASSESSMENT

Grading kids on their best work and none of the rest.[42]

---

[40] You may have noted that we spelled esteem wrong on the previous page. We got so upset when the editor pointed it out that he agreed not to make us change it. We argued that you readers would certainly know what we meant anyway. Thanks to a really neat editor, we feel much better about ourselves.

[41] During our years of research for this book we asked many teachers what it meant. Our favorite response was:"Oh hell, I don't know. It's one of those terms you hear all the time but don't pay any attention to."

[42] Time was when Vermont farmers dreaded the day the "milk inspector" showed up (twice a year mostly unannounced) to inspect the stable and milk house. The idea was to insure that milk was produced—day in and day out—in clean barns. This was the old "pop quiz" method. Portfolio assessment of dairy barns would go like this. You get a letter that reads:"Why don't you get your place cleaned up the very best you can? In other words go all out and get really spiffy. Call in the neighbors to help if you want. Then call us when you're ready and we'll come over and inspect it." Under which system would you rather drink milk?

THE COMMON CORE

You don't want to know. Trust us on this. Like what goes into sausage and lawmaking. . . it's not a pretty picture.

STANDARDS-BASED EDUCATION

Used to be called "basic competencies," which was junked for the new term when the old one became too associated with what educationalists call the extreme right wing, *i.e.*, people who actually believed in basic competencies. In the lala land of educational jargon, "standards" means setting a goal that every student can pass. If they can't, you are allowed to "adjust" the standard. It's like "flexible standards," but the cheating comes first. All this to smooth the road to Lake Wobegon.

Culturally Normed
Exam Questions
(For Vermont Students)

To learn what students know, educators say it's important to ask them questions in a language they understand. Thus daughters and sons of ranchers in Montana, native Americans in New Mexico, inner city kids in New York, Appalachian mountaineers in West Virginia, and so on all demand exams written in local dialects. (*Dontchuno.*) The educationalists, of course, need to jargonize this phenomenon. They call it "cultural norming." To make sure Vermont kids are not disadvantaged by exams written out of state, we have written a few culturally normed questions for Vermonters. For instance:

SOCIOLOGY 101 (True or False)

Out of State Question

Urban sociologists agree that maximizing infrastructure investment will lead to increased traffic flows, elongated shopping patterns, urban decay syndrome, and the eventual depression of regional quality of life indexes.

True_____ False_____

Vermont Normed Question

Wal-Mart sucks.

True_____ False_____

AMERICAN HISTORY 101 (Multiple Choice)

Out of State Question

Historians generally agree that a myriad of forces combined to create what Professor Ipile Alottabull calls a "causal chain reaction" of socio-economic and political variables leading to the Civil War. The most important of these forces was:

_____A.   The demise of the Whig Party, which led to the election of Lincoln.

_____B.   The reliance of the South on a uni-dimensional economic structure featuring agriculture.

_____C.   The opening of the West, which raised the slavery question in the new states.

_____D.   Increased Australian cotton imports to the European Continent.

Vermont Normed Question

What caused the Civil War?

_____A.   Slavery

_____B.   Slavery

_____C.   Slavery

_____D.   Slavery

POLITICAL SCIENCE 101 (Essay Question)

Out of State Question

In your readings and in class lectures you have been introduced to a concept called "Paradoxical Presidents." Discuss how the following elements of this notion relate to our choices of presidents in America: 1) The Electoral College which gives big states like California 54 votes for President and states like Vermont only three; 2) Presidential Ambition Theory, which indicates that those most anxious to become president have least success in being president; 3) Ideological Coherence Theory, which suggests that most successful presidents demonstrate a clear linkage between party label and issue positions; 4) "Counterfeit Candidates" (usually governors of small states) who gain national recognition by abandoning their duties while in office and use the electoral process to publicize their own ego. (30 minutes)

Vermont Normed Question

Why did Howard Dean waste a year running for president on our dime? (30 seconds)

16

Who Ya Gonna Call?

(Understanding the Chain of Command)

Let's suppose your child, though very bright and brimming with self-esteem, can't read a Berenstain Bears book upon entering high school. What do you do?

Call the **governor's** hot line.

He'll say he can't do any thing. The Board of Education is in charge.

Call the **Board** of Education.

They'll say the Commissioner implements policy. All they do is think up new ideas.

Call the State **Commissioner** of Education.

You'll be told the State Department of Education has all the power.

Call the State **Department** of Education.

No one there will know anything.

48

*Vermont
Owner's
Manual*

Contact your **local school board**.

They'll say arrange a meeting with the superintendent of schools. (She's the one at the end of the table who looks like she makes $80,000 a year.)

Go to see the **superintendent** of schools.

She'll send you to the principal.

Go to see the **principal**.

The principal is very busy. He'll send you to the classroom teacher.

Go to see the **teacher**.

The classroom teacher will meet with you and your kid, a counselor, assistant principal, special assistant for home school coordination, and member of the state's internal affairs committee.

Go see your **kid**.

Apologize.

17

The Education Rules

From the time Vermont's Constitution urged every town to build a schoolhouse, Vermont has maintained one of the most inclusive, democratic, and progressive public school systems in the free world. But this tradition is being threatened. Your *VOM* offers the following rules to help us stay on track:

- ⚑ Good teachers detest bureaucracy more than you do.

- ⚑ Vermonters know the difference between being stupid in a clever kind of way and clever in a stupid kind of way.

- ⚑ Self-esteem *follows* accomplishment.

- ⚑ The school superintendent makes more than you do.

- ⚑ Vermonters never confuse feeling with thinking.

- ⚑ Any curriculum that doesn't involve learning how to tinker isn't worth a damn.

- ⚑ The very worst teachers in your school will be paid as much as the very best. Exactly.

- ⚑ Any parent going to watch their kid play an outdoor sport in either the spring or fall is in danger of dying of hypothermia.

▼ Any exam that can't be failed shouldn't be taken.

▼ If it clouds up any day between November 15 and April 15, it's a safe bet they'll close the school.

▼ A good grade school teacher is worth more than a good high school teacher and certainly more than a good college teacher.

▼ The school system wants your kids. Politicians are willing to give them to it. The teachers don't want any part of that. They want to teach. Let them.

▼ War, a wise man once said, is too important to be left up to the generals. Education is too important to be left up to the educationalists.

18

The Act 60 Page

We hear now and then from nay-sayers who complain about Act 60's complexity. We disagree—it's easy to understand! To demonstrate, we present Montpelier's latest formula for the Act's impact:

$$VOA60=[(BP)+((\sum_{i=1}^{i=n}(G))-(\sum_{i=1}^{i=n}(B))^2]-(GMP)+\sqrt{JDIQ}$$

Where:

VOA60 =	Value of Act 60
BP =	Bonus Points for Act 60
G =	Good stuff about Act 60
B =	Bad stuff about Act 60
GMP =	Giggle Meter Points
JDIQ =	Justice Dooley's IQ

TO FIND WHAT THE BENEFITS OF ACT 60 WILL BE FOR **YOUR** SCHOOL, PLEASE TURN TO PAGE 63.

19

Sacred Cows and Baler Twine

(Living with the Farmers)

No conundrum complicates the operation of the new (post-family farm) Vermont as much as the following:

IF FARMERS ARE SO IMPORTANT TO THE OPERATION OF VERMONT, HOW COME THEY DON'T ACT RIGHT?

Here's the problem. Farmers (real ones) *like* pesticides. They like doing things the *easy* way.[43] They like to kill stuff too. Corn (when it's ready). Trees when they're ready.[44] Crows, hens. They'll even gun down a cute little fox terrier or poodle if they catch it running deer in the spring. In late August (at dusk) they're apt to gun down the same deer themselves and put it in a freezer.[45]

Most of all farmers like to do things their way. Flatlanders are surprised at this.

That's why they're called flatlanders.

---

[43] Flatlanders do too, but only after they've tried throwing bales *up* into a hay mow (the damn fools) instead of figuring a way to push them off a wagon *down* into a hay mow.

[44] Or the price of lumber makes them ready.

[45] Sometimes they poison *woodchucks* (for goodness sake)!

The farming way of life is a way of independence, personal judgment, no bosses, and facing the *consequences* of one's actions. That is what George Aiken meant when he said that a fierce sense of liberty and "living up among the hills"[46] are reinforcing attributes of the farming life in Vermont.

Here's the key. You want to save the hill farm? You want hillside Jerseys and valley Holsteins? You want high pastures and meadow hedgerows? You want that exquisite mix of wood and field on which is formed the essence of traditional Vermont topography?

If so, having farms is a necessity.

To have a state where farmers abound.
Is to have a state (if democracy's sound!)
Of governments grounded in local dominion
And citizens full of feisty opinion.

---

[46] We have always loved Aiken. How many other Vermont governors wrote a great book (*Speaking from Vermont*) too? He, among very few, described Vermont farmers as living *among* the hills. What genius; to tell us that Vermont is so hilly that one family, living on 150 acres (more or less) still lives *among* hills rather than *on* a hill. What a difference a preposition makes.

Farmers are *not* optional.

Coming to Grips with the New Agriculture

It used to be that fish food was canned mud worms in the back pocket of a barefoot farm boy. Now it's highly caloric ice cream named after a rock band[47] sold to bring peace to the world.

It used to be the most sophisticated part of the tractor was the power take off.[48] Now it's the air conditioning. It used to be manure was shoveled and then *spread* in the spring when it mixed in nicely with the brown fields of March and April. Now it's pumped and then *sprayed* onto green grass (which it burns to a crisp). You got used to the smell of the old stuff. It was a harbinger of spring.[49] The smell of the new variety is so bad it drops meadowlarks in full flight.

It used to be the only traffic congestion getting in and out of Rutland, Brattleboro, or Burlington (or any of Vermont's larger places) was caused by cows crossing the road. Now photographers have to *search* for such photo ops. In fact we know one farmer who suggested he might sell them by hiring a local kid in a straw hat and dungarees to deliberately run his herd back and forth

---

[47] It's *Ben and Jerry's* "Phish Food."

[48] No, no, no! Tractors don't fly. (Flatlanders!) It's using the engine's power to turn a shaft that runs a hay rake, baler, or (years ago) a circular saw to block up four-foot wood.

[49] Vermonters were so desperate for spring in those days, aged cow manure became an aroma.

across the road."Probably make more on that than I can on the milk," he said.

It used to be "diversity" in Vermont meant a mixed herd—Holsteins for quantity, Jerseys for butterfat count,[50] Guernseys to look good at the fair, and Ayrshires to keep you alert during milking. Now diversity means raising carrots, llama trekking, selling Christmas trees, lambing, or changing your farm into a golf course.[51]

It used to be we had to hopscotch the cow "pies" and cow "flops" when walking Vermont meadow land. At least no bakery or shoe manufacturer has commercialized these terms![52] Now the cows are kept in sanitized, temperature-controlled free stalls[53] and milked in "parlors," where they are visited by smaller herds of school children on "field trips." It is oddly disquieting, busing school kids through rural Vermont to be guided through dairy barns in groups. Your Vermont cannot be operated properly if the only agriculture we have is advertised as follows:

[50] This was in the days when butterfat was considered *good*.

[51] Although no one who has not milked cows 1,624 days in a row morning and night gets to complain. (Even when they mark distances on their driving range with Holstein cutouts.)

[52] But candy makers have! Our editor's kid got one, described as a "cowpie chocolate thingy," in his stocking at Christmas. Apparently, it was the one piece of candy not consumed. Smart kid.

[53] It's funny how these oxymorons keep popping up.

CHEAPER BY THE HERD[54]

HEAD TURNING . . . GIANT SIZED COUNTRY COWS

A FUN WAY TO DECORATE YOUR YARD

Get ready for the compliments when you set up these friendly Country Cows—they'll bring country charm to any yard or garden. Imagine, these Giant Sized, Black and White Cows peering out from under your trees, shrubs, or from your lawn. They'll make a "head turning" impression even from afar! Realistically posed each single piece cut-out has been crafted from all EX-TERIOR GRADES Materials. Comes with Garden Stakes already attached—just press into ground. They measure about 2 feet across. Start with one or round up your own herd—our special, multiple prices are very low.

One Cow	$5.88
Two, only	$11.00
Three, only	$16.00
Six Country Cows, only	$30.00

Ground Stakes Attached

Weatherproof Exterior Made

Crafted from a Solid Piece

Painted Black and White

[54] As advertised in national magazines.

58

Vermont Owner's Manual

We leave you with a notation that sums up the challenge:

> "Those who labor in the earth," said Thomas Jefferson, "are the chosen people of God." Vermonters know that's an exaggeration—of sorts. Vermont without farmers could be a good place too but it could never be Vermont; and while there are lots of good places, there is only one Vermont. Ever since Vermont began, those who worked the land have defined our every contour—the economy, the politics, the villages and towns, indeed the very landscape that enwraps our lives. The chosen people of God? Maybe not. But close, very close.

And with the words of Victor Davis Hanson, from his *Field Without Dreams*. It presents an ideal that too many Vermont politicians seem to abhor at the same time they claim to revere farmers and the landscaped paradise that two centuries of painful life bequeathed to us:

> Is there another besides the ugly agrarian whose voice says no to popular tastes, no to the culture of the suburb, no to the urban enclave, no to the gated estate? What other profession is there now in this country where the individual fights alone against nature, lives where he works, invests hourly for the future, never for the mere present, succeeds or fails largely on the degree of his *own* intellect physical strength, bodily endurance, and sheer nerve?[55]

Where indeed?

[55] Victor Davis Hanson, *Fields Without Dreams* (New York: The Free Press, 1996) p. xii.

20

Comments of Previous Owners

It is hard in this day, in which the American tempo is so speeded up, to sit back and be comfortable with what you have. It requires education and culture to appreciate a quiet place, but any fool can appreciate noise. Florida was ruined by that mania. It must not happen in Vermont. You have priceless heritages—old houses that must not be torn down, beauty that must not be cluttered with billboards and hot dog stands. You are guardians of this priceless heritage and you are fortunate to have the honor of that task instead of being horn-blowers.

Sinclair Lewis, Barnard, 1929
(First American to receive the
Nobel Prize for Literature)

When a person makes the change from city living to country living, he becomes involved in situations and conditions which could not possibly be foreseen—as a result of these unforeseen contingencies, many of the experiments in rural living made in Vermont have ended in disaster and disillusionment . . . yet those who failed in country living failed because they were unwilling or unable to change their **basic scale**[56] *of values.*

Sam Ogden, Landgrove, 1952

---

[56] Emphasis our own.

Now in the big silence of the snow is born, perhaps, not a little of the New England Conscience, which her children write about. There is much time to think, and thinking is highly dangerous business. Conscience, fear and undigested reading ... have full swing. A man, and more particularly a woman, can easily hear strange voices—the Word of the Lord rolling between the dead hills; may see visions and dream dreams; get revelations and an outpouring of the spirit ... Hate breeds as well as religion—the deep, instriking hate between neighbors, that is born of a hundred little things added up brooded over, and hatched by the stove when two or three talk together in the long evenings.

Rudyard Kipling, Brattleboro, 1893

(British author who wrote the *Jungle Books, Captains Courageous,* and *Kim* in Brattleboro.)

21

The "High Chair" Treatment
(Crime and Punishment)

Despite the fact we are blessed with one of the most law abiding populations in the civilized world,[57] there are "rules of the road" that must be followed. In Vermont, of course, they are often not what they seem and they are seldom like those of other states. In Vermont it is *legal* to pass on a solid line.

Here the penalty for a crime can be issued by a tribunal of your neighbors (it's called "community sentencing"). Vermont is one of the few states with a "good Samaritan law." It is a *crime* to stand around and do nothing when someone's in trouble. Vermont is the only state in which you don't have to go to law school to practice law. It is here that the search for justice is often aided by a unique system of "lay judges."[58] Vermont has no death penalty. We have no maximum security prison.

---

[57] Not counting jacking deer, the "mail box game," or growing your own.

[58] New arrivals to Vermont often make the mistake of equating this with a special court system (analogous to a "family court") that deals specifically with crimes of passion.

In truth, however, our penal code and the way we enforce it reflects another fundamental truth: hard living among the hills calls forth a justice of human scale defined as "There but for the grace of God go you or I." It all began with the Green Mountain Boys. They defeated New York and the British Empire without killing a single person. A lot of people got drunk at Ticonderoga. Nobody got killed.

It was during this time that the "High Chair" Treatment was instituted as the quintessential punishment by shame. Putting someone in the stocks was uncomfortable, and now and then a dog might pee on them. Therefore offending sheriffs from New York were tied into chairs and drawn high into the air over the village green. There they swayed to and fro, mightily mortified but safe and comfy.

To avoid the "High Chair" Treatment pay close attention to the following.

What's a Crime? What's Not?

In Vermont there are legal crimes and illegal crimes. Driving your pickup with its agricultural plates into town for a movie is a legal crime. Watering the maple syrup is an illegal one. Dropping a nice fat doe in the middle of the new potatoes in August is legal as long as you keep your mouth shut about it. Shooting one in May for the hell of it is a felony. Skinny dipping's ok. Public nudity's not. Dogs caught tearing a woodchuck to pieces are ignored. Dogs caught doing the same to a deer are executed on the spot. Howard Dean going on more than twenty

𝔓age 63.

minutes in a high school graduation address is a misde-
meanor. For Jim Jeffords it's a felony.

There are also activities that are legal in some places
but illegal in others.

LEGAL IN WOLCOTT AND ILLEGAL IN WOODSTOCK

▼ Letting your cat have kittens

▼ Shopping at a Wal-Mart

▼ Covering your wood pile with plastic

▼ Making less than $50,000 per year

▼ Driving a pickup with a gun rack in the window

▼ Owning a dog without a pedigree

▼ Opening a Laundromat within sight of the highway

▼ Having a mailbox shaped like a cow

▼ Parking a parts car on your front lawn[59]

▼ Painting your house purple with orange trim

▼ Using a bug zapper

▼ Owning a 1987 Chevette

[59] In Woodstock even having a parts car is illegal.

LEGAL IN WOODSTOCK AND ILLEGAL IN WOLCOTT

Aside from having a French poodle or a Ph.D. in political science, ***nothing*** that's legal in Woodstock is illegal in Wolcott! (Though forcing people to work during deer season would probably qualify too.) That's what's great about living in the Kingdom. Freedom.

22

Green Up Daze

We haven't inherited this land from our ancestors;
we have borrowed it from our children.

—Haida saying

Use it up / Wear it out / Make it do / Or do without.

—Vermont saying

There is one area where all Vermonters from Swanton to Brattleboro and from Canaan to Pownal need to reach agreement—the environment. The key, of course, is population control. Trouble is, this leads to bumper stickers like "Welcome to Vermont. Now Go Home" — hardly befitting our tradition of kindness and tolerance.

Less openly offensive is the hidden agenda of many newcomers known as the "gang plank syndrome" ('Now that I'm here, let's keep everyone *else* out!'). This often shows up in planning documents and zoning schemes that mean prices so high that only the affluent can afford to live here.

One Out—One In

(Your *VOM*'s Preferred Environmental Policy)

Over a decade ago we offered the perfect solution, a "One Out, One In" policy based on the creation of a limited number of "Vermont Passports" issued to all Vermonters as

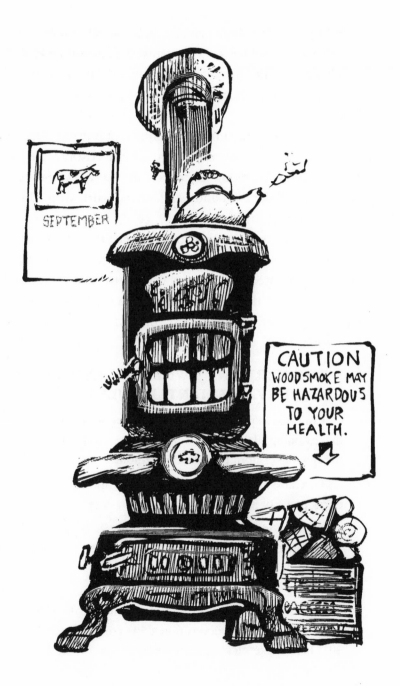

68

a birthright and proof of citizenship.Those silly enough to leave Vermont could give them away,will them to their kids, or sell them at a flea market or garage sale.But no one could *move here* unless a passport became available and they obtained it.

Our plan had the unique advantage of putting a market value on "life in Vermont" through the cost of a passport (call it a "Vermont Share") on the New York Stock Exchange.Think how handy such an indicator would be around election time!

The only thing we had to do to put this ingenious scheme in place was to secede from the Union,something a lot of Vermonters have always wanted to do anyway.

Unless and until Vermonters are willing to secede from the Union, the next best thing is to observe the following rules.

THE VERMONT OWNER'S MANUAL
ENVIRONMENTAL RULES

Continue to pave over Chittenden County and hope that by piling all the people on top of one another there the rest of Vermont can remain Vermont.

Purchase a "Return to Sender" stamp and use it on every piece of junk mail you get.

What good is cross-country skiing if you use a two-ton gas-guzzler to get to a touring center? Use the pasture out behind the house.

Double the deposit on returnable bottles to a dime. Back in the 1950s a Coke was a nickel and the deposit was 2¢.At that rate a deposit on a 50¢ coke should be 20¢! Let's make picking up the empties *profitable* for the kids again. And think what it will do for the purchase of new basketball uniforms for the junior high girl's basketball team.[60]

Don't dilute the problem by equating "beauty" with a clean environment. Let the chucks have their junks. Wait until they park them in the river, then arrest them.

Get used to it. Cow manure may smell, but it's *wicked* pure (*dontchuno*).

No new roads anywhere, anytime, for whatever reason!

Oh no you don't. No new roads disguised as "improvements" either. Let the roads curve and meander among our hills. Remember what you love this state for! The idea is not to get from Saint Johnsbury to Montpelier ten minutes quicker by taking the bends out of Route 2. The idea is to enjoy the trip.[61]

Every third child you have must become a farmer.

---

[60] Unless, of course, the Supreme Court rules it unconstitutional for kids to earn money that way because it discriminates against those towns that are sober and clean. After all, how can a child be penalized for having parents that won't move to a town where the roadsides are strewn with litter?!

[61] Besides, a couple of years after making the road swift and straight it'll draw enough new traffic to take up the original ten minutes saved and cost you an additional five to boot. Only now you'll be looking at more tailpipes and breathing more exhaust. If politicians who live in St. Johnsbury and want to get to Montpelier quicker don't like it, let them move to Montpelier.

No off-road motorized vehicles can be used except for work or dragging out a moose. Roaring indiscriminately through the fauna of field and forest on an August afternoon is not recreation. It's a crime.

With VAST leading the way, snowmobiles are OK.

Riding lawnmowers must go the way of billboards. We all can use the exercise.

23

The Politicians
(Who to Let Operate
Your Vermont)

The politicians are the ones we allow to *operate* Vermont. They do the things we need done in common. Consider them people you'd let *drive* if you were dozing in the back seat. In the days of Nixon we used to ask, "Would you buy a used car from this man?"Your *Vermont Owner's Manual* asks,"Would you let these people drive your car?"[61]

PATRICK LEAHY?
A drugstore cowboy in a fake ten-gallon hat driving us to a Grateful Dead concert?

CHERYL RIVERS?
That's all we need, a band of loggers from the Kingdom smashing the car to bits with a sledge hammer for $5 a pop.

MICHAEL OBUCHOWSKI?
A chauffeur who looks like a walrus! We'd end up on an ice floe in James Bay. (*Ferchrissake*)[62]

---

[61] Or run your chain saw or milk your cows?

[62] If he'd only shave the mustache, he'd be the best looking pol in Montpelier.

HOWARD DEAN?

Look at his record! He tried to drop us off at a *Motel 6* and drive off by himself to Washington to become President. Remember?

JIM JEFFORDS?

Here's a guy who's spent thirty years in a Republican car driving on the Democrats' side of the road. He's so busy dodging and swerving, no wonder he makes us sick!

BERNIE SANDERS?

Talk about road rage.

RUTH DWYER?

Who needs a driver whose favorite gear is reverse?

JIM DOUGLAS?

Every time the traffic gets heavy or the pavement's damp, he'll pull Vermont over and wait for better conditions.

JOHN McCLAUGHRY?

He'd pull a U-turn and drive against traffic all the way back to 1800, his favorite year in American history.[63]

JACK McMULLEN?

Before you can drive in Vermont, you have to live here long enough to get a Vermont driver's license.

DOUG RACINE?

You wanna spend the rest of your life in an Isuzu or Jeep on a trip with no destination?

---

[63] He might even stop off at the Alamo on his way back to 1800. The guy loves massacres. Look what happens to him every time he runs for office.

PETER SHUMLIN?

Never let anyone drive your car who wants to too much.

SUSAN SWEETSER?

She won't drive unless she's nursing a baby. Talk about an accident waiting to happen.

FRED TUTTLE?

Good man. Bad plan.

JIMMY "ICEMAN" DEPIERRO?

He's a member of the Vermont "Grassroots" Party. He's got ice in his name and grass on his mind. Ice and grass. It sounds like he'd at least understand Vermont.

WHO SHOULD GET THE KEYS?
TURN TO PAGE 63.

24

Surviving Deer Season

If you have three or more dogs sleeping on your front porch, you may skip this section. If you think the term "road hunter" is just another Vermont put-down for a lost tourist or a deer run is held on St. Valentine's Day in the streets of Burlington, read it carefully:

FLAG

A deer's tail is brown on top and white underneath. When a deer runs, it becomes a bright white *flag* bouncing through the woods. *Flag* can be a noun, "I saw some *flags* but didn't get a shot"; or a verb, "I *flagged* a few but didn't see any horns." If you are out raking leaves and see one of these flags, dive under the porch.

A DRIVE

A *drive* has nothing to do with leaf peepers on Sunday afternoons. It's worse: a gang of Vermonters plowing through a thick patch of woods to *drive* the deer out the other side, whereupon another bunch of Vermonters will start blasting away. If you wander into the middle of a *drive, park* yourself behind a tree. A big one.

ROAD HUNTING

A *road hunt* is unrelated to a *drive*. It's lazy hunters in a pickup truck cruising back roads hoping real hunters will scare deer out into a field or across the road. If the truck is moving, you're safe. If it *stops* in front of your place, throw yourself to the ground and pray Muffy's in her doghouse. If you are following *road hunters* in your car, they will pull over to let you pass. Do so.

A RUB

In the early fall bucks rub their antlers on saplings to rid them of the skin that covered them during the summer. This leaves a clearly visible bare spot on the little tree. The bigger the rub, the bigger the buck. Hunters like to sit downwind from a rub ready to shoot. If you ever happen on a rub while walking in the woods in November,[64] raise your hands (slowly) to your mouth, cup them, and scream: "I don't have any goddamned horns!"

A STAND

A *stand* is a place where hunters *sit* (or *lean* against something). It is a few yards away from a place where, in a hunter's best judgment, a deer may soon be passing by. Never stand near a *stand*. But if you must, don't move. Not even an inch.

A RUN

A *run* has nothing to do with the "Covered Bridges Half-Marathon" or "Kaynor's Sap Run." It is a heavily traveled path through the woods—for deer. Deer never run on *runs*. They *walk*. In November they *sneak*. Until spotted by a hunter. Then they *run*. Like hell. Never walk on a *run*.

THE RUT

The *rut* is the time in the fall when does come in heat. Bucks become cantankerous (actually damned angry) if their courtship is interrupted—and imprudent. Accordingly, hunters love

---

[64] Anyone crazy enough to go on a walk in the woods in November should probably move back to Paramus anyway.

the *rut. VOM* has no particular advice to give you on the matter of the *rut* except for the following true story. One fall a Vermont bow hunter plastered himself with doe scent, climbed into a tree, and waited. Sure enough, along came a buck. The hunter shot it and jumped proudly from the tree. Unfortunately, he still smelled, well, amorous. That is when the second buck arrived, mistook him for the first buck, and damned near killed him. Don't say we didn't warn you.

POSTING

Because people post their land to keep hunters off, you may think it is safe to walk through the woods on posted land. It's not.

Here is the *VOM*'s top ten list of things one should **never** do during deer season:

- Walk a Great Dane
- Cough outdoors.[65]
- Whip out a white handkerchief to blow your nose.[66]
- Climb a tree in a black jacket.[67]
- Step into an open field at dawn.
- Step into an open field at dusk.
- Ask: What's that long flashlight for?
- Stand near a "Deer Crossing" sign.[68]
- Move suddenly.
- Step into an open field at any time.

[65] It sounds like a buck snorting

[66] It looks like a *flag, dontchuno.*

[67] Deer season overlaps with bear season—**black** bear season.

[68] Or a "Bear Right" sign. Flatlanders often take up *stands* near them.

25

Are You Ready to Operate Vermont?

Quiz #3

(Your Third Chance to Demonstrate
Your Vermont Aptitude)

One thing every Vermonter must know (almost by instinct) is the difference between Vermont and New Hampshire. Let's see how you do.

1. Vermont has higher taxes than New Hampshire.[69]
   ____ True ____ False

2. New Hampshire owns the Connecticut River.
   ____ True ____ False

3. On which of the following does Vermont exceed New Hampshire?
   A. Population
   B. Height of the Mountains
   C. Area in Square Miles
   D. Number of State Legislators

---

[69] We thought we'd start you off with an easy one.

4. The Federal Government owns more of Vermont than it does of New Hampshire.

_____ True _____ False

5. Which state   VT   NH
    A. has colder Februaries?   ___   ___
    B. voted for Roosevelt in 1936?   ___   ___
    C. has more lawyers per capita?   ___   ___
    D. is the home of *Yankee* magazine?   ___   ___

6. Who said the following?

"Anything I can say about New Hampshire can be said as well about Vermont. Excepting they differ in their mountains. The Vermont mountains stretch extended straight: New Hampshire mountains curl up in a coil."

    A. Ethan Allen
    B. Robert Frost
    C. Henry David Thoreau
    D. Daniel Webster

Answers: 1. True
2. True
3. Area
4. False
5. (A) VT; (B) NH; (C) VT; (D) NH
6. Robert Frost

26

Yeas and Nays
(Coping with Town Meeting)

Town meeting is one of the most important events of the year for a Vermonter. But it may be difficult to understand. This is because people confuse "pure" democracy with "perfect" government. If we want perfect government, we should elect a philosopher king and be done with it.

Town meeting is real democracy. It reflects communities of real people, warts and all.[70] It is assembled passion. Sometimes dormant, often aroused. Its most important function is not the passing of laws but rather the training of citizens. But it cannot train citizens unless they can pass laws which themselves may be wrong. Real laws with real consequences. In short, town meeting must give citizens enough power to make mistakes.

Town meetings are dreaded by authoritarians, avoided by cynics, and cherished by democrats. Here are some dos and don'ts for town meeting day:

▼ Never vote to adopt the Australian ballot for any reason whatsoever.

▼ Never criticize the road crew.

[70] Thus it fits our favorite description of democracy. "It is like sex. When it is good, it is very, very good. When it is bad, it is still better than anything else."

79

▼ Always pretend to listen when your state representative comes to address the meeting.[71]

▼ Never begin a speech with the words "before I get to the principal thrust of my remarks, let me say this…"

▼ Never give a "speech."

▼ But if you really must, *never* clear your throat first.

▼ If the governor shows up, don't be in any hurry to let him (or her) speak. Finish what you're doing first. They're only after votes; you're practicing democracy.

▼ Never follow a flatlander who has just finished his first "speech" in town meeting on some silly motion to do some silly thing by yelling: "So move!"[72]

---

[71] Unless they go on for more than 15 minutes. After that time you may fidget all you want.

[72] They might think you want them to leave town!

Time and Action

Issue	Time	Suggested Action
To authorize the selectmen to borrow money in anticipation of taxes.	5 seconds	Pass it. They'll do it anyway.
To appropriate the Fire Department $5,000 per their request.	10 seconds	Pass it. Reverently.
To approve the Road Commissioner's request for $250 to repaint the grader.	3 hours	Kill it. Too expensive.
To appropriate $728,426 to meet the expenses of the town for the ensuing year.	15 seconds	It's only money.
To move the town meeting to Monday night at 7:00 p.m. and place all money items and election of town officers on an Australian ballot to be voted on the following Tuesday.	Take as much time as you like.	Just make sure you kill it.[73]

[73] Then put it in a twenty-quart lard pail, fill the pail with cement, take the first ferry from Burlington to Port Kent, and heave it overboard in a deep spot near the New York shore.

Time and Action

Issue	Time	Suggested Action
To increase the tax rate for schools by 20% to meet new expenses, provide for updated computers, and establish a new music program.	Give it a moment of silence.	Give it another moment of silence. Education is being separated from our Democracy by Act 60.
To ask our Senatorial delegation in Washington to deliver the following resolution to the President without delay: *The Town of Marlboro hereby warns the President of the growing danger of the Christian Right and calls for an executive order prohibiting any right wing Christians from sleeping in the Lincoln bedroom.*	5 seconds	Sand down a rat hole. Give it five seconds and pass it.

Town Meeting Glossary

ITEM	WHAT TO DO
The Warning	This is a published list of items to be discussed at town meeting. Often the Selectboard will *warn* a meeting improperly and everything you do is moot. Many times this is a *good* thing.
The Australian ballot	Refer to footnote #73.
Unfunded Mandates	Fight 'em.
Robert's Rules of Order	Obey them, no matter how foolish they seem.
New Business	This is when you thank the cooks for lunch—unless it's getting late.
Tabling	You "table" a well meaning flatlander's proposal to establish a committee to study an "adopt a pasture" program. You KILL the Australian ballot (see above).
Cutting Off Debate	It's like corporal punishment. Use it rarely and gently.
The Office of Fence Viewer	Combine with the office of Hog Reeve and Weigher of Coal and give the position to a newcomer.

THINGS TO BRING ALONG

❧ A seat cushion

❧ Ear plugs

❧ Patience

❧ Your knitting

❧ Common sense

❧ An appetite

❧ Intolerance for verbosity

❧ A sense of humor

❧ The Town Report

❧ Lunch money

❧ Tums[74]

❧ A capacity to suffer damn foolishness

Town Meeting: The Great Leveler

In 1975, just a few months after local hero Tom Salmon of Rockingham scored a stunning upset at the polls to become governor of Vermont, he returned home to attend the annual town meeting. Bright and articulate, Governor Salmon knew he was on sacred ground and

---

[74] More and more towns are serving quickie food during the meeting, rather than taking the time to adjourn for lunch and sit down to a good old-fashioned town meeting dinner. (We know of one town that actually brought in "Dunkin' Donuts." We are not cruel enough to reveal which one.) Many towns still serve such dinners. If you don't live in one, it may be worth quitting your job, selling your place, and moving to a town that does.

he limited his involvement, listening to the debate and voting on the issues. But near the end of the meeting, he rose to defend a proposal to increase a town officer's pension. Surely, he thought, a short word from the governor—a citizen of the town returning in triumph—carried some weight. It did not. Nay![75]

Before he died in 1991 Dick Snelling had served more terms as governor of Vermont than anyone since before the Civil War. After his death this most famous of Shelburne's citizens and former star in the firmament of Vermont and a player on the stage of national politics earned a moment of silence during the Shelburne town meeting. Receiving equal time (heads were bowed for both at once) was Mrs. Ellwood, a citizen who had served the town in various capacities, but who was not a public figure outside of town. Shelburne gave them both its most honored requiem—a simple moment of silence together, as equals.

Democrat or Republican, man or woman, local worker, governor, or president of the United States, town meeting plays no favorites. All persons are equal before God, the Constitution, and Robert's Rules of Order.

[75] To his great credit Tom Salmon relates this story to this very day as testimony to the efficacy of town meeting.

27

Comments of Previous Owners

I never drive up the valley from Bennington to Arlington, watching the glorious chains of mountains march ahead of me, that I do not think of Carl's Marching Mountains symphony ... He needs no recording of his symphony, in one sense, because centuries, millions of them, have already recorded it in the everlasting contours of Vermont's mountain beauty.

Margaret Hard, Arlington[76]

Go west, young man, go west.

Horace Greeley, East Poultney[77]

[76] Margaret Hard, *A Memory of Vermont: Our Life in the Johnny Appleseed Book-shop* (New York: Harcourt, Brace and World, 1967). She is referring to Carl Ruggles.

[77] It was John L. B. Soule who wrote these exact words in an editorial in the *Terre Haute* (Indiana) *Express,* but he was just editing the prose of Horace Greeley, the great Vermont essayist, lecturer, and editor (*The New York Tribune*), who understood how tough life can be in beautiful spots. Greeley prefaced his famous "go west" dictum with the following from his essay *To Aspiring Young Men:* "The best business you can go into you will find on your father's farm or in his workshop. If you can't do that," he advised, "turn your face to the great west." When Greeley was growing up in Vermont young men (and women too) couldn't and did.

The record of Vermont as a resolute champion of individual freedom, as a true interpreter of our fundamental law, as a defender of religious faith, as an unselfish but independent and uncompromising commonwealth of liberty-loving patriots, is not only unsurpassed, but unmatched by any other state in the Union.

George Harvey, Peachman[78]

Vermont is the most glorious spot on the face of the globe for a man to be born in provided he emigrates when he is very young.

Stephen Douglas, Brandon

[78] Harvey was publisher of *Harper's Magazine*.

28

Governors and Hog Reeves
(Who do you vote for?)

Voting is more than a right in Vermont; more than a duty. It's an obsession. We elect more statewide officers than almost any state in the Union. We elect 180 legislators in Montpelier to do the business of 600,000 people. California elects 120 to do the work of 33,000,000. We elect fence viewers and justices of the peace and constables and hog reeves and tree wardens. We elect our statewide officials every two years instead of every four like the other states. Voting correctly, therefore, is obviously essential to a smooth running Vermont. Here are some guidelines to help fulfill your duty as an owner and satisfy this special Vermont passion.

FIRST CONSTABLE
Vermonters never elect a constable who weighs less than 450 pounds.

ROAD COMMISSIONER
Vote for someone living on your road.

TOWN LISTER
Vote for someone who doesn't know you have a cellar or an attic or (better yet) doesn't even know where you live.

SCHOOL BOARD

Never vote for anyone who is named Heidi or Shane, earns more than $70,000 a year, comes from California, or has a graduate degree in education.[79]

TOWN AUDITOR

Take the first unsuspecting newcomer.

TOWN MODERATOR

Elect the second most trusted person in town.[80]

TOWN CLERK

Chose the *most* trusted person. She or he will know more about your family than you do,[81] must be politically astute, very, very smart, and also capable of identifying the body parts of various kinds of wild game.

GOVERNOR

Anyone living outside Chittenden County ought to get special preference.[82] Never vote for a candidate for governor with a name that starts with "B" and ends with "sanders."

[79] A school board member must have the wisdom to see through the bureaucratic bull the administrators use on the one hand and the guts to face down enraged taxpayers on the other. They must be willing to work hundreds of hours (often at night) for 6¢ per hour only to be told by state officials that they don't know what the hell they are doing anyway. This is the office we have in mind when we use the term public *servant*.

[80] It also helps if they can suffer fools but not pretension, have read Robert Frost's "The Death of the Hired Man," possess a booming voice, and have to be home for chores by 4 p.m.

[81] Actually they may know more than *you* want to know about your family.

[82] For nearly forty years (with only a couple of exceptions) our governors have lived in either Shelburne or Burlington.

STATE REPRESENTATIVE IN MONTPELIER

Vote for anyone who puts conscience over party line and who will never forget where they came from; that is, a *town*.

SELECTPERSON

A selectperson must know trucks. That's about it.

PLANNING COMMISSIONER

You don't vote for them. That's the problem.

ZONING ADMINISTRATOR

Get someone who doesn't want the job.

CONGRESSPERSON

Bernie. He's out of state, relatively harmless, and can rant and rave to his heart's content. He makes liberals feel good about themselves and gives conservatives something to worry about. Everybody wins!

29

Neighbors

Even before Robert Frost penned his historic line *Good fences make good neighbors* in "Mending Wall," neighbors had a special status in Vermont. It comes from the geography. It calls individualists but requires cooperation.

In the old days (prior to 1950 and after 1840), the chief neighbor problem was a lack of them. Most of them moved out. A lot went to the large towns down by the depots. More moved to the flatlands of the Midwest.[83] Those who stayed were well known entities, since they and their ancestors had lived on the same farm (next to your place) forever.

Now things are different. A steady stream of new neighbors has been arriving since the 1960s. It's all very confusing. The newcomers want to be good neighbors but they don't understand that to be one, you've got to, well, **back off** for goodness sake. And Vermonters have got to understand that in the post modern world, neighbors can be useful for something besides helping rebuild a barn!

The first thing to do is to identify their status. For instance, if the new neighbor's little girl has a gun rack

---

[83] Vermont led America in out-migration during this period.

Imagine that. Real Vermonters traveling 1,000 miles to become flatlanders. Life had to be tough here to cause that.

on the back of her tricycle, you know immediately with whom you're dealing. When the first thing off the U-Haul[84] has a gasoline engine and tracks, you will probably not be asked to loan out last week's edition of *Barrons*.

On the other hand, if the new neighbors ask you over for a "get acquainted supper" within the first week, you know you've got a job on your hands. If the husband's first name is the name of a town, or they carry a pooper-scooper when they walk their dog,[85] or they have a bumper sticker that reads *If men got pregnant, abortion would be a sacrament* or *Rush Limbaugh for President,* be prepared for trouble.[86]

For Woodchucks

Let's face it. Sometimes you gotta fit in. You're invited to a party of wall-to-wall flatlanders. It's held at the Whitcomb-Merryweather's. Bradley makes a living from home that involves a ton of out-of-state mail. Veronica (Ronnie) is a lawyer in town.

What's wrong with leaving the twelve-gauge at home? Better yet, take the gun rack out of the pickup for the evening. Or park the damn thing and take your husband's

---

[84] Flatlanders never drive U-Hauls or Ryder trucks. Their stuff arrives in a moving van the size of Howard Dean's ego. They show up several days later in air conditioned Volvos.

[85] *Crimus!* If they walk their dog at all you know you've got a flatlander to deal with.

[86] It's not *what* they believe. It's *how* they believe it.

car. How much is that going to hurt? Suppose someone named Tiffany says something like this: "I wish those red-necks down the road would resolve their masculinity anxieties and stop killing those beautiful deer." You don't **have** to say, "Spit out the veal cutlet, you hypocritical wench, or I'll send Buster out to get my 300 Remington and we'll see how fast you can run in those Birkenstock sandals!"

Lay off. You're big enough. We're all Vermonters.

For Flatlanders

Suppose you're new in town and you're invited to a barbecue at the Johnsons, a long-time Vermont family controlling seven town offices, 1,272 acres of land, and the EMS crew. Their front yard features a fishing boat parked right beside the pink flamingo guarding a bathtub Madonna. So what if they don't have bottled water. There's always a chance the spring is above the house. Drink up.

And eat the damn hot dog. One won't kill you.

If Beth Johnson's husband Hank cocks his thumb at the flag on his jacket and says, "I pray t'God every night that someday one of them long-haired weirdos tries to burn this one here," you could say, "You Twinkie-glutted neanderthal. The Constitution that protects those 'weirdos' also keeps the rest of us from passing a law making it illegal to utter trite, banal absurdities in the company of people with sense!" But don't.

Leave it be. Go with the flow. We're all Vermonters.

30

What Do You DO Up There?

Even as a citizen in Vermont you will probably travel out of state for short periods of time. Almost anywhere you go, you will be an object of curiosity, even amazement. On the street, in convenience stores, or at toll booths, people will ask: "What do you **do** up there?" It's helpful to have an answer prepared so you won't have to think about it. Therefore, your *Vermont Owner's Manual* is happy to provide a few geared to the mood in which you find yourself and the tone you wish your response to generate.

WHAT DO YOU **DO** UP THERE?

YOUR MOOD	*VOM* SUGGESTED RESPONSE
Cautious	"Are you a game warden?"
Stereotypical Yankee	"None of your damn business!"
Sarcastic	"My favorite good time is the scavenger hunt for the annual road-kill church supper."[87]

[87] The 1998 winner was Walter Wheeler of Hyde Park, who brought back a slightly decomposed Vietnamese Potbellied Pig he found on the Mountain Road in Stowe. 1997's winner was a Columbian Wirehaired Coco cat Mildred Stone found on Route 12 just south of Woodstock.

WHAT DO DO UP THERE?

YOUR MOOD	*VOM* SUGGESTED RESPONSE
Feisty	"I raise Mexican Hairless dogs. What's it to you?"
Pessimistic	"Whatever. It'll probably snow anyway."
Cryptic	"The gods of the hills are not the gods of the valleys."
Dumb	"Why don't you come up, buy a place, settle down, and find out for yourself?"
Ornery	"Any damn thing we want."

31

Flatlander Syndrome
(Recognizing the Early Warning Signs)

Flatlander Syndrome (FS) is becoming Vermont's most serious psychological disorder. Insurance companies are being called to include it on their "pay-out" list of treatable diseases. After having spent several years committed to becoming real Vermonters, newcomers are especially susceptible. But woodchucks are at risk too. It creeps up on them as insidiously as property taxes and extra weight around the middle.

There is no way you can operate your Vermont correctly if you catch it. So your *Vermont Owner's Manual* offers the following tips for early detection and the chance for a permanent cure.

Suppose you're a real Vermonter who married a flatlander named Reggie from Delaware. He's trying hard to become a real Vermonter—an owner—like you. But he requires constant attention. Then *you* start feeling strange. Could you have caught it from Reggie? Conditions around you are perfect for the disease. First they built a golf course out of the Simpson Farm. Next the diner was replaced by a bagel shop. Now none of your kid's playmates understand your mom's accent when she comes down from Hardwick to baby sit.

Then just last week your development voted to amend its covenant to prohibit clothes lines in the yard and you felt no outrage. OHMYGOD. It *is* FS!

Don't panic. Early detection is key. Here are some proven remedies:

Call a real Vermonter and beg her to take you to deer camp in the fall. Pay her if you must but find a way to go.

Buy an old bathtub, paint it purple, and put it in the front yard. If your neighbors complain, tell them to stick it. It's *your* front yard, and this is Vermont.

If you live in Chittenden County (where FS is pandemic) spend next Saturday as follows:

1. Go to yard sales in the morning
2. Drive up to Tatro's Auction House in Alburg in the afternoon. Lunch on diet coke and jelly donuts (those nice half dozen packs) on the way.
3. Finish the day with supper and dancing at the Charlemont in Morrisville. Get a room at the motel so you won't have to drive home. Drink a lot of beer.

Buy a snowmobile and join VAST.

Go ice fishing on Lake Memphremagog.

Write a letter to the editor of the *Rutland Herald,* call for an open season on moose, and threaten to bring Satan down on the editorial board if they don't approve.

If you live in southern Vermont, attend the flea market in Wilmington next weekend and follow that up with dinner at the Chelsea Royal Diner in West Brattleboro.

If there is a bottle of wine in the house that costs more than $5.00, pour the damn thing down the toilet!

Say *shee-it* at least three times a day.

Get yourself a bumper sticker that reads "I love animals. They're delicious" and put it on your car.

Go to town meeting and vote "no" on at least three requests from out-of-town, not-for-profit organizations. Make sure they are for good causes. It'll drive the flatlanders nuts. They'll pass anyway so you can't do any real harm. But everyone in town will at least *identify* you as a Jedi *chuck*.

Recommit to accepting no more BS from any FS afflicted politicians, doing everything you can to protect *your* right to have some real say on the common decisions that affect your life, and keeping Vermont clean and *livable* for your kids. After all, isn't that what you're fighting FS for in the first place?

If you have trouble taking these remedies, spend a weekend in Secaucus, New Jersey. That'll give you the commitment you need.

If you do these things recovery should begin before you know it. You may find yourself slowing down near swamps on early April evenings and listening for peepers again. Or you may discover you owe more on your snowmobile than your car! Perhaps you'll find yourself back at Agway looking for 200-pound sacks of dog food. When you hear your neighbor won the lottery you automatically think he got a moose permit. Or you will realize you no longer worry about the trash in your neighbor's back yard. Then you'll forget to lock your car again. These are all *wicked* good signs that you are on the road to recovery.

RECOGNIZING THE EARLY WARNING SIGNS OF FS

If you haven't ever contracted FS, the following are symptoms that can warn you that you may have been exposed.

- You see a bumper sticker that says:"Adjust? Hell No! Fight It!" and don't have a clue.
- Your mom's cat Buster turns twenty and you go to a vet instead of doing the job yourself.
- While shopping for a new car you ask:"Does it have a sun roof?"
- You drive down wind by a barnyard and say: "peeyew!"
- You listen to a speech by Al Gore.
- It makes sense.
- You post your land.
- You think a good night out is a "Bed and Breakfast."
- An advertisement for land in Florida attracts your attention.
- You drive by a hitchhiker on the Stannard Mountain Road.
- Senator Jim Jeffords tries to put some passion into a speech and you keep a straight face.

▼ You have pancakes at a friend's house in Massachusetts and don't mind the Log Cabin.

▼ Senator Patrick Leahy releases the amount of out-of-state contributions he took to get reelected and you don't barf.

▼ You take the old washer off the front porch and put it in your shed.

▼ Bill Clinton says something and you believe him.

▼ A snowmobile roars under the window at 3 a.m. and you mutter an obscenity.

▼ A woodchuck takes up residence in your garden and you call "Friends of Varmints Removal Service" instead of blowing his ass off with your twelve gauge.

The Quintessential Symptom of Flatlander Syndrome

You think Exit 12 (Taft's Corners) of Interstate 89 in Williston is a

▼ *SCENIC OVERLOOK* ▼

32

Are You Finally *Set to Operate Vermont?*
Quiz #4

The most practical and impressive skill in operating your Vermont successfully is knowing how to get around. Think of the adoration you'll receive from family and visitors alike when you *head out up over* the Bethel Mountain Road *along down through into* Bethel and you actually *end up* in Bethel.

1. To get from Brandon to Rochester you take:
   - A. Route 4
   - B. Route 9
   - C. Route 73
   - D. You can't *get* to Rochester from Brandon

2. To get from Brattleboro to Halifax you take:
   - A. Route 9
   - B. Interstate 91
   - C. The Molly Stark Trail
   - D. You can't *get* to Halifax from Brattleboro

3. Which of the following towns is not in the North-east Kingdom?

    A. Bloomfield

    B. Cabot

    C. Brighton

    D. Coventry

4. Match the town with the river that flows through it. (Nail this one and you're in!)

A. Sharon	1. Nulhegan
B. Arlington	2. West
C. Bloomfield	3. Missisquoi
D. Newfane	4. Batten Kill
E. Enosburg	5. White

Answers:

1. C

2. D   In fact you can't get to Halifax from Brattleboro unless you want to take the Jacksonville Stage Road that takes you almost to *West* Halifax and then on to Jacksonville (which is a "place" by way of the Branch Road and Route 112).

3. B   Cabot (in Washington County) is right on the border. It just doesn't quite make it.

4. A = 5; B = 4; C = 1; D = 2; E = 3.

33

"The Gods of
the Hills"

YOUR VERMONT WARRANTY

To determine what Vermont guarantees you,

TURN BACK TO PAGE 63

34

Safety Features

Remember those 1957 Chevrolets? A billion horse-power and no safety features. Then they came out with "padded dashes," followed by shatterproof glass. Now we have seat belts, airbags, anti-lock brakes, and spring-loaded bumpers. Fortunately, Vermont, too, has a pretty long list of safety features, most of which come standard.

LONG MISERABLE WINTERS
Known as "Darwin's Deliverance," it sends the weak of spirit back home. It's the surest population control device now available.

NOSEEUMS
They teach us the ultimate uselessness of chemical antidotes.

VERMONT LIFE MAGAZINE
Vermont's drug of choice.

MUD SEASON

A reminder of the power of nature and the fragility of muffler pipes.

THE TWO-YEAR TERM

It's like an emergency brake. We almost never have to use it to make a change, but you never know.

THE VERMONT CONSTITUTION

Ignore it today and what happens when you need it tomorrow?

THE VERMONT HISTORICAL SOCIETY

In Vermont more than any other state: "We are what we were!"

JOHN McCLAUGHRY AND MURRAY BOOKCHIN

Every society needs a John McClaughry and a Murray Bookchin, and we've got good ones.

CHITTENDEN COUNTY

A constant reminder of what not to do with the rest of the state.

THE ACLU

Like McClaughry, we need it. It's part of our conscience.

EARLY ADJOURNMENT

Sometimes it's good to stop and think.

35

Optional Features and Spare Parts

These are things we can do without. Although not necessary to properly operate Vermont, they might come in handy now and then, even though in some cases it's hard to imagine why.

- ▼ The Republican Party
- ▼ Montreal[88]
- ▼ The President of UVM
- ▼ Stowe[89]
- ▼ The State Department of Education
- ▼ New Hampshire[90]

---

[88] There's nothing wrong with city life as long as it's in someone else's country.

[89] What would we do without Stowe and all the sales, gas, liquor, and rooms and meals taxes it generates? Besides, Stowe is packed away up there in a valley north of Waterbury mostly out of sight.

[90] It provides tax-free shopping for Vermonters who live along the Connecticut River. It maintains the bridges and provides educational and medical facilities we can use. Most of all it provides the gutless with a nearby alternative where they can still freeze to death.

- The Auditor of Accounts
- Manchester Center
- Milton[91]
- The Lieutenant Governor
- The Berlin Mall
- Ruth Dwyer[92]

[91] With Hardwick gentrifying, we'll probably need it. But if Husky wreaks too much havoc Milton may start to look like the rest of Chittenden County. Then where will we be?

[92] She drives the governor nuts.

36

The Vermont Weather Page

Vermont's weather seldom kills you outright. We have few catastrophic floods, tornadoes, forest fires, or earthquakes. In Vermont the weather is like April. It tortures you to death in a flirtatious episode with a love that will remain forever unrequited. In his book *Vermont, A History*, Charles Morrissey says of Vermont's weather: "A Vermonter may conclude, without fear of paranoia, that getting from Thanksgiving to Memorial Day can be cruel and unusual punishment."

TWO MORE COMMENTS ON THE WEATHER

To one born in the west, where grass does not make turf except in high pasture meadows, the cropped sward of a Vermont ... pasture has a touch of the paradisiacal about it ... as well as a reminder of boyhood trips into the wilderness. Though rains are frequent and often torrential [in Vermont] which lies under the St. Lawrence storm track, the good days are like the good days in the western mountains. The light is intense, the deep sky is crossed by navies of fair-weather, strato-cumulus clouds, the horizons are cut with a diamond, the air has never been breathed. And those days come so infrequently between days of clouds and rain and violent thunderstorms, and

*are spaced through such a brief and fragile time,
that a man believes he deserves them and has a right,
because of what else he has to put up with, to enjoy
them thoroughly.*

Wallace Stegner, Greensboro, Vermont[93]

*Of the twenty-six storm tracks crossing the coun-
try on their way to the Atlantic Ocean, twenty-three
pass over Vermont. Consequently Vermont weather
changes every few days the year round, and the Vermonter faces the biological necessity of constantly
adjusting his body to rapidly alternating heat and
cold, high and low barometric pressure, and seasonal
changes of humidity and air ionization. Every such
adjustment to climate must be made by a change in
the blood circulation. One day the skin is called upon
to be a radiator, giving off heat. The next day it may
have to be an insulator, retaining body heat. This
puts a great strain on the heart and blood vessels.*

Dr. DeForest C. Jarvis, Barre, Vermont[94]

For the answer to what you can do about the Vermont weather,
TURN TO PAGE 63

[93] Wallace Stegner *The Uneasy Chair: A Biography of Bernard
DeVoto* (Garden City, New York: Doubleday & Company, 1974)

[94] From his book, *Folk Medicine: A Vermont Doctor's Guide to
Good Health.*

37

Don't Brake for Field Mice!

(The Commuter Rules)

It used to be Vermonters' biggest road problems were manure spreaders, road hunters, and Route 7. Now things are different. We commute more and enjoy it less. So far road rage is limited to folks like Ruth Dwyer listening to WVPR or Howard Dean waiting at a railroad crossing behind a car with a "Ruth Dwyer for Governor" bumper sticker. But beware—the road culture is changing for the worse. Below are rules to help keep you safe and sane on the road.

While Driving to Work, DON'T

- Let more than two dogs ride in the front.
- Pass a *dubblewoid* on a corner.[95]
- Rubberneck at moose.
- Leave the yard until you've scraped off a frost hole as big as your credit card.
- Be the *second* driver to hit the skunk.

---

[95] *Mother* says it's *wicked* dangerous *dontchuno.*

111

Vermont road culture

- ☛ Panic if your GPS says you're in the Northeast Kingdom.

- ☛ Gesture obscenely during Terry Gross interviews or Rush's rantings.

- ☛ Freak out if a mouse pops out of your heater.

- ☛ Get upset at the arthritic cow crossing the road in front of you.[96]

- ☛ Speed up to nail the crow having lunch on the white line.[97]

- ☛ "Sight in" your 30:06.

- ☛ Let your Pekinese sit on your shoulder or your kid in your lap.

- ☛ Knit at the wheel on Interstate 89 or 91.[98]

- ☛ Pass on a double line. It's legal, but it's nuts.

- ☛ Leave home without your chainsaw.[99]

- ☛ Laugh at the SUV sliding backwards on the black ice onto the median of I-91.

- ☛ Stop for road kill before dark.

---

[96] There's one in every herd.

[97] You'll never get the clever bastard anyway.

[98] Really! A friend of ours swears she saw a knitter at the wheel on I-89. "Knit one, pearl two, BRAKE!"

[99] Especially after a high wind.

38

The Best of Everything

To own Vermont one has to *know* Vermont. As more people are drawn to Vermont, newcomers, visitors, tourists, and family "from away" will inevitably ask questions like: What's the best place to find ginseng? Where's the best espresso bar in Newport? Some you don't have to answer. (What's the best county for big bucks?) Others you wait years for. (What's the best way to get to Glover from here?)[100] Here is a list of possible questions and some suggested answers.

WHAT IS THE BEST? THE ANSWER IS:

Day of the year?	January 4th. It's really the most dreadful day of the year, which means it's all downhill from there. *A day without dread is about as good as it gets in Vermont.*
Cow?	Any of 'em nowadays.
Place to find turkeys?	Anywhere in Chittenden County.

---

[100] Prepare for this! (See Quiz #2 on pp. 38-39.) The key is to keep your cool. Chances are you'll not get more than one or two chances in a lifetime.

WHAT IS THE BEST? THE ANSWER IS:

Radio Station? WDEV in Waterbury: Hands down.[101]

Car in the snow? A 1987 Chevette with two grain bags in the back. The "front wheel drive theory" proved mythical. It's okay for flatlanders' driveways. But to blast through the deep stuff, it takes a little engine in front, a lot of weight in back, speed, and a primeval scream: "What the hell. It's only a 1987 Chevy!"

Parking Garage? Rutland.

Commercial Airport? We've only got one.

Politician? It's still George Aiken, and he died years ago.

Dance Hall? It's still Cole's Pond in Walden, and it burned down.[102]

Ice Cream? Sewards.[103]

Auction House? The Alburg Auction House.

Cemetery? Hope Cemetery in Barre.

Sunset? Mt. Philo.

[101] The three best radio programs ever produced in Vermont also came out of WDEV. They were: *Don Field and the Pony Boys* circa 1950—live country and western music; *Once Around the Clock* with Rusty Parker—a trillion drops of milk filled pails during morning chore time to the sounds of this program; and Brian Harwood and Ken Squier's *Music to go to the Dump By,* which went the way of the seagulls when open dumping was discontinued.

[102] The Bay Side Barbecue in Saint Albans comes close, however.

[103] Gotcha!

WHAT IS THE BEST?	THE ANSWER IS:
Trout Stream?	Find your own.
Day Hike?	Camels Hump. Any trail will do.
Opera House?	Haskell's in Derby Line.
Dog?	A beagle/lab cross.
Route to New Hampshire?	Who cares?
Ski area?	Mad River Glen—it's owned by the people.
Run[104]?	Covered Bridges Half-Marathon.
Honey[105]?	Bill Mares's! (Hey, it's our book.)
Newspaper?	*The Green Mountain Trading Post*— located in the Kingdom town of Charlestown. Its motto is "no news is good news." Instead you get poems and essays by local people and pages and pages of stuff for sale. It offers what it calls "check-cashing money" for short stories and poetry.[106]

---

[104] For fish it's the Willoughby River for steelheads on the meadow just below the old high school in Orleans.

[105] The kind bees make. For the human variety, it's still Lola Aiken.

[106] In a recent issue the following were listed for sale: A Quick Lay Boring Machine; Fire Hydrants; A Bug Guard; Old Shooters Bibles; A Juke Box; A Harpoon Hay Fork; A Gas Toilet; Two Medium-Sized Pigs; John Deere "H" Parts; Mini Donkeys; A 486DX 66W/8mb RAM, 400 h/d floppy; An Oliver OCY Crawler; Justice of the Peace Services—Weddings Anytime, Anywhere.

WHAT IS THE BEST?	THE ANSWER IS:
Sunrise?	Ascutney.
Country Fair?	The Orleans County Fair in Barton. It used to be Tunbridge before the flatlanders took over.
Flea Market?	Wilmington.
Poet?	David Budbill.
Humorist?	Justice John Dooley, for the *Brigham Decision*.
Museum?	There are two of them. The Ethan Allen Homestead in Colchester and the Fairbanks Museum in St. Johnsbury.[107]

---

[107] Why are there two? Because this book has two authors, that's why.

39

Comments of Visitors and "Summer People"

Drive up one side of the Connecticut River and down the other side. The New Hampshire side has been shrewdly developed with all known devices to attract the tourist trade. The Vermont side is barren of them: it is not only a different landscape, it is a different organization of society.

Bernard DeVoto, American historian.
Editor of *Harper's*
Morgan, 1936.

They hewed this state out of the wilderness, they held it against a foreign foe, they laid deep and stable the foundation of our state life, because they sought, not the life of ease, but the life of effort for a worthy end.

President Theodore Roosevelt
on a trip to Vermont in 1902.

Under their frozen exterior no other people were more kindly, friendly, neighborly, and good to know, and I think I could cite no other community in this country with an equal variety of the permanently sterling. In truth, these people wore their austerity as they wore their painfully formal Sunday clothes, in obedience to tradition unmeaning and inept; if they were close bargainers they were usually

*upright; and if day by day they seemed absorbed in traf-
ficking they sedulously maintained a standard of general
culture, high and rare.*

Charles E. Russell.
Nationally known essayist,
social reformer, and progressive.

*[Vermont] ... abounds in the most active and most re-
bellious race on the continent and hangs like a gathering
storm on my left.*

British General John Burgoyne
on his way down Lake Champlain to
his defeats at Bennington and Saratoga
and the end of British rule of America.
(The British never ruled Vermont.)

40

The Media Page

As a joint owner of Vermont, you are responsible for knowing what's going on—what's happening to your Vermont. It used to be the local telephone operator could tell you. Vermont didn't extend much past your own town. Now it does.

To find out what's happening:

- ☞ Read the *Burlington Free Press* to find out less about more of what happened.

- ☞ Read the *Rutland Herald* to find out more about less of what happened.

- ☞ Watch the "**Channel Three News Hour**" to see fifteen minutes of what happened stretched into sixty.

- ☞ Log on to www.vtdemocrats.org to find out what the Vermont Supreme Court will require to happen.

- ☞ Log on to www.vermontgop.org to find out what most hope will never happen.

- ☞ Read the *Brattleboro Reformer, Bennington Banner, St. Albans Messenger,* and *Newport Express* to find out *part* of what happened.

- ☞ Read **Peter Freyne** to find out what happened to someone who wished it hadn't.

- ☞ Check out the *Caledonia Record* to read "It happened . . . whatta ya goin' to do about it?"

- Read *Behind the Times* to find out why what happened happened.

- Listen to **Vermont Public Radio** or read *Vermont Life* to feel good about what happened.

- Watch **"Vermont This Week"** to see journalists spin what happened.

- Read the *Ethan Allen Institute Newsletter* to find out what John McClaughry hopes will happen.[108]

- Read *Vermont Magazine* to find out what's happening to Vermont's *nouveau riche*.

- Read the *Upper Valley Herald* to find out what happened in the old fashioned way.

- Read the Vermont Historical Society's *News and Notes* to find out what used to happen.[109]

- Hang out in the **Statehouse cafeteria** to hear the politicians tell you what woulda, shoulda, coulda happened.

- Watch **"You Can Quote Me"** if you don't care what happened.

- Listen to **WDEV in Waterbury (550 AM)** and discover that "what's happening" really doesn't matter much anyway. It'll make you feel good. Trust us.[110]

---

[108] But probably won't.

[109] And many wish still did.

[110] You *can* find out what happened at Thunder Road and the Montpelier-Randolph girls basketball game or discover how many moose are going to get shot in the fall or where the hot yard sales are for the weekend. The real stuff.

41

Vermont Political Correctness

In Vermont political correctness is viewed with suspicion. It should be. We have always been the most politically *incorrect* of states. It was in Vermont that the first anti-Christian book ever published on the North American continent was published by (you guessed it) Ethan Allen, a man who today could be the love child of Sinead O'Connor and Pat Buchanan.

Vermont was America's first frontier! Here people came to be given the liberty to be politically *incorrect* (as long as they didn't make a nuisance of themselves or infringe on anyone else's right to be as much of a damn fool as they were). When the Mormons and the Pilgrims of Woodstock and the New Lights of Hardwick and the Meliorates[118] and the Shakers and the Nudists[119] and the Free Lovers wanted to be left alone, they came to Vermont.

PRESENT-DAY VERMONT POLITICAL CORRECTNESS

▼ Never go through a coin drop without contributing.
(If you lose the receipt, pay up again.)

---

[111] Founders of the Seventh Day Adventist Church.

[112] Nudists! Vermont is freezing nine months of the year and black fly infested two of the other three. They *had* to be weird!

NUDE SHAKERS
BLUEGRASS
CONTEST

▼ Never honk your horn at slowpokes.

▼ If you run for public office, never speak ill of your opponent.

▼ Always sit in awe at a public meeting when real farmers speak.

▼ Never take anyone's picture without asking first.

▼ Never turn anyone in for burning a little grass.[113]

▼ When a woman is elected selectman, call her whatever *she* wants.

▼ When the zoning board meeting is over and someone says,"We need some help putting the chairs back under the stage," don't head for the door. Who the hell are you, anyway?[114]

▼ Gay marriage? Consider the position of Mrs. Patrick Campbell, who at the time of Oscar Wilde's trial reportedly remarked:"I don't care what they do as long as they don't scare the horses in the streets." There's a dictum Vermonters can live and let live with.

[113] Any kind of grass.

[114] If you *really* have an excuse (your husband is due to come out of open heart surgery in half an hour), the best bet is to pretend to go to the ladies room and then slip out another door.

42

Which Road to Take?

Two roads diverged in a wood, and I—
I took the one less traveled by,
And that has made all the difference.
"The Road Not Taken"
Robert Frost

These three lines were penned in New Hampshire (of all places!) by a California native more than eighty years ago. And yet they have touched a nerve in generations of Vermonters. Simply living in Vermont involves choosing a road less traveled.

But Vermont is at a crossroads. The siren call of current American culture washes over Vermont every day, telling us that we should want everything big, easy, less personal. The red carpet is out, the road is smooth, the convenience of it all is tempting. But the Vermont way has never been the easy way. For all the rewards it offers, the road is bumpy and difficult. Traveling it takes effort and care.

Ethan Allen, Thomas Chittenden, and the rest set Vermont on this road, forging a whole new republic in the face of appalling pressure from the outside. Now it's up to us to face the pressure and decide our future. Which road do you want to take?